In August 1986, the Army Lynx demonstrator, G-LYNX, broke the absolute world speed record for light-medium helicopters, previously held by the Mil A-10 (development version of the Hind). A speed of 215 knots (398k/h) was recorded on an approved course near Glastonbury in Somerset. In Norway, G-LYNX (also with the military serial ZB500 to enable weapons to be carried) was used for TOW trials in cold weather. (Westland)

ATTACK HELICOPTERS

Paul Beaver

ARMS AND ARMOUR PRESS

Contents

First published in Great Britain in 1987 by Arms and Armour Press Limited, Link House, West Street, Poole, Dorset BH15 1LL.

Distributed in the USA by Sterling Publishing Co. Inc., 2 Park Avenue, New York, NY 10016.

Distributed in Australia by Capricorn Link (Australia) Pty. Ltd., P.O. Box 665, Lane Cove, New South Wales 2066, Australia.

British Library Cataloguing in Publication Data:
Beaver, Paul
Attack helicopters
1. Military helicopters –
History I. Title
623.74'6047 UG1230

ISBN 0-85368-742-0

Jacket illustrations: Front: fitted with the research probe on the nose, the A129 has been put through an exhaustive period of test flying. The first deliveries to the Italian Army are scheduled for 1987 and the first unit should become operational in 1988. (Rolls-Royce) Back: supporting Sagger-armed BMP (armoured personnel carrier), the Soviet air force, including fixed-wing Fencer aircraft, provides Hind-D support. In theory the helicopter's thermal-imaging capability should allow the aircrew to 'see' through the smokescreen laid to cover the advance. (TASS via Mike Gething)

All British Army, Royal Air Force and Royal Navy photographs included in this book are British Crown copyright.

Designed and edited by DAG Publications Ltd.
Designer: David Gibbons.
Editor: Michael Boxall. Layout artist: Anthony A. Evans.
Typeset by Typesetters (Birmingham) Ltd. Printed and bound in Great Britain.

Unveiled at the 1982 Middle Wallop Air Day, the Lynx-3 is an improved, enlarged and uprated version of the Army Lynx. The helicopter's basic equipment includes a night vision sensor on the nose, a mast-mounted sight, exhaust collars and the Westland BERP blades.

Introduction

Helicopters were first introduced to the battlefield during the Korean War of 1950–53. Of the many roles in which they have proved their worth since then, none is more demanding – and more beneficial to an army commander – than that of the 'attack helicopter'. This book takes a highly illustrated look at the current attack helicopter scene, and the development of the concept which has led to the advanced helicopters now under development for service in the late 1990s and the 21st century.

First, though, we must adequately define the term 'attack helicopter' which in turn will set out the limits of this book. During the last 40 years, many terms have been used to define the helicopter that carries troops to the battlefield, or which directly supports those helicopters in 'fire teams' and other collective terms. The dedicated combat helicopter with the direct fire role is still a rare beast among the armed forces of the world, and depending on a country's political, financial and technological abilities, the attack helicopter has been variously defined as: anti-tank helicopter, assault helicopter, anti-armour helicopter, combat helicopter, armed reconnaissance helicopter, scout and attack helicopter. This book sets out to cover all of these by dealing with:

1. Armed reconnaissance of the battlefield.
2. Early developments.
3. American attack helicopters.
4. European developments.
5. Soviet assault helicopters.
6. Future concepts.
7. Future developments of the attack helicopter.

According to the leading trade journal of the military helicopter industry, *Defence Helicopter World*, there are 6,820 attack helicopters of various types currently in inventory, on order or in reserve. This figure, which represents about 25 per cent of the world's military helicopters, includes scout, observation and utility types which can be armed and have been seen to be so during the past few years; in addition, the data for the Warsaw Pact nations is estimated from the best sources available. These helicopters can be identified in the accompanying data tables. Before reading this book, the following facts ought to be borne in mind.

The first documented deployment of attack helicopters was made by the French armed forces during the Algerian war (1954–62) using the Sikorsky H-34 Choctaw built under licence in France. This helicopter mounted a variety of weapons including early Giat 20mm cannon and unguided rockets. At about the same time, the US Army had begun to follow up its Korean experience with the development of rocket-propelled grenades and other weapons fittings to the Bell H-13 Sioux.

INTRODUCTION

The first dedicated attack helicopter in production was the Bell AH-1G Cobra which entered service with the US Army in Vietnam during 1967, following experience gained with the Huey armed utility helicopter.

The Soviets developed their first armed assault helicopter, the Mi-24, called Hind by NATO, in the late 1960s with a service entry date of about 1972. It was not until 1983 that the first European-designed and built attack helicopter, the Agusta A129 Mangusta made its first flight.

By the year 2000, the US Army expects to have at least 2,000 specialized attack helicopters in service, backed up by the McDonnell Douglas AH-64A Apache and the remaining Bell AH-1S Cobra types.

Development of the attack helicopter has only just begun.

For the light attack role, the Apache can be configured to carry 70mm rocket launchers, although it is more usual to see Hellfire missiles on the inboard pylons. The 30mm chain gun is standard to whatever weapons fit has been specified.

Armed Reconnaissance of the Battlefield

Knowing what is over the hill has been a primary requirement of all battlefield commanders since before the Romans. In recent centuries, mounted light cavalry, kites and balloons have been used to spy out the land, and during the First World War, it was the aeroplane which took on the role of observation across enemy lines. Autogyros being out of favour during the Second World War, it was not until the Korean conflict that the US Army developed a requirement for a light observation helicopter (LOH) to take on the role which had been fulfilled by mounted scouts during the various US conflicts of the nineteenth century, thus giving the LOH the name 'scout helicopter'.

The scout helicopter comes under the guise of several different names but for the purposes of this book, we shall examine those directly involved in the support of attack helicopter fire teams, flank protection and fire direction, as well as those which themselves are armed – a much rarer situation. Although the Bell 47 was used in large numbers by the US armed forces and some 35 other nations for liaison, communications and light observation, it was not until the development of the larger, turbine-powered helicopters that the US Army was able to run a competition for the first Light Observation Helicopters (LOH), to replace the existing Bell H-13 (Bell 47) and Hiller H-23 helicopters as well as the Cessna O-1 light observation aeroplane.

In 1961, the LOH competition was staged with the Bell OH-4 (later to become the OH-58 Kiowa), the Fairchild-Hiller OH-5 (later the FH-1100/RH-1100M) and the Hughes OH-6 Cayuse which was declared the winner in 1963. The first production run of the OH-6 (later to be known as the LOACH in Vietnam) was for a little over 700 helicopters and in about 1968, with the war in South-East Asia requiring a massive US injection of arms, equipment and men, the LOH competition was re-run and this time the OH-4 was selected in its improved OH-58 version (similar to the US Navy training helicopter already in production).

The OH-58A (which led to the frequently seen Bell 206 JetRanger family) was ordered in quantity by the US Army, with the first production run of 2,200. In recent years, the OH-58A has been superseded in its fire team scout role, usually undertaken with Cobra attack helicopters, by the improved OH-58C version which includes mountings for light machine-guns and the General Dynamics Stinger air-to-air system.

In 1981, the US Army confirmed its intention to improve the existing scout helicopter support to be given to the forthcoming advanced attack helicopter programme, the AH-64A Apache. Bell Helicopter Textron, the manufacturer of the OH-58A from 1968 to 1973, was awarded the contract for the Army Helicopter Improvement Program (AHIP) to upgrade some 578 Kiowas from A and, later, C standards. The new AHIP design is a high-technology development of the basic airframe which includes new Allison 250-C30R engines, the mast-mounted sight, laser designation for the Apache's Hellfire anti-armour missiles, and cockpit displays from TV (CRT) screens. The OH-58D entered limited service in 1985, but being such a complex helicopter some development work was required before it could be fielded alongside the first Apache battalions from Fort Hood (Texas) in 1986.

In Europe, the United Kingdom and France had developed both light observation helicopter requirements and the design proposals to fulfil the army staff requirements. Initially, the designs were for unarmed or lightly armed observation types, but the Westland Scout and the Aérospatiale Alouette III gradually developed into light anti-tank/attack helicopters. In the United States, the Kiowa range were also armed with wire-guided anti-tank missiles and took on an attack role; these projects are discussed later.

As a result of various large-scale army exercises, including 'Lionheart' in 1984, it has become apparent that the forward units operating helicopters need at least some form of self-defence, such as a gun or lightweight launch-and-forget missiles, and even a means of attack. The armed reconnaissance helicopter concept calls for lightly armed attack helicopters to penetrate to the very edge of the forward battle area (FEBA) to identify targets for the direct fire arms on the battlefield – field artillery, tanks, infantry equipped with ground-launched anti-tank weapons and of course the attack helicopter. In the United States, the various Bell developments of the OH-58, including the TexasRanger and Combat Scout, have been bridging the gap between armed scout and attack helicopter, with some export success. Many of the light attack helicopter designs, such as the Rogerson-Hiller RH-1100M Hornet, have the potential to attract overseas buyers, particularly for less intensive warfare in Central and South America.

Bearing in mind the Sikorsky maxim that all Soviet helicopters encountered on the battlefield are armed, the light scout types, such as the Mi-2 Hoplite family (all built in Poland and variously developed by that nation's helicopter industry), have to be treated with care. It is known that all Mi-2 are built with gun mountings, ammunition chutes and positioning flanges, and in recent years a number have been photographed with light anti-tank missiles, again indicating that this lightly armed scout bridges the gap between the pure scout/observation and light attack helicopters. Although there are possible developments with the Mi-34 scout-trainer which entered production in 1986 and of which no illustration has yet been released, the Soviets have concentrated on larger, more potent attack helicopter concepts typified by the Mi-24 Hind series and later developments.

1. Highly successful in Vietnam, the Hughes OH-6A Cayuse is no longer in service with full-time US Army units except for the Special Operations Command. The 300 or so in the US Inventory are operated by the Army National Guard Aviation or the US Army Reserve. Although designed as a four-seater, performance and comfort are better with two crew, a pilot and observer. (McDonnell Douglas)

2. Operated without doors during active service in South-East Asia, the Cayuse was occasionally armed with light machine-guns, including the 7.62mm mini-gun, but more often flew with Cobra 'Snake' teams in an attempt to draw enemy fire by low flying; the Cobras waiting to engage the enemy with rocket and cannon once the hostile fire position had been established. (McDonnell Douglas)

▲3 ▼4

3. The Cayuse's success led to further development of the design in the civil helicopter field, and the licensed production by Breda-Nardi in Italy (the latter now being part of the Agusta Group). The Breda-Nardi NH 500 series includes a scout armed with two 7.62mm guns and an 18-round 70mm rocket launcher; other light weapon combinations are possible. (Breda-Nardi)

4. For looking over the hill, the 500MD Defender series was fitted with the Hughes Aircraft Corporation mast-mounted sight which has a television observation sight system. It is possible to use this aid for passive observation for long range, but it is more usual to fit a wire-guided anti-tank missile system, like TOW, for attack purposes. Other light fire suppression weapons can be fitted. Again, this is an example of bridging the gap between light armed observation and attack roles. (Breda-Nardi)

5. Built for the US Army in large numbers, the OH-58A Kiowa remains in widespread service, especially with US Army Europe (USAREUR) forces where the helicopter is used for flank security, close support (with 7.62mm mini-guns) and fire team coordination. (Author's collection, 35mm)

6. To improve the capability of the US Army's fire teams, especially with the introduction of the Apache, the (US) Army Helicopter Improvement Programme or AHIP was commenced in the early 1980s and has meant the conversion of a large number of OH-58A to OH-58D Aeroscout standards. The ball-like mast-mounted sight includes provision of laser range finder and designator for Hellfire helicopter-launched missiles and the Copperhead artillery shell, as well as low-light television and infra-red sight. This enables the OH-58D to operate equally well by day or by night. (Bell)

7. The cockpit of the OH-58D has been fully integrated with all the available electronic systems and has the ability to hand-off data for an attack task to the attack helicopters in company with it. In combat, the helicopter would be 'down among the weeds' in nap-of-the-earth flight, a few metres above the ground, and would be armed with the Stinger air-to-air guided missile to protect itself and the attack helicopters it would be supporting. (Bell)

5▲

6▲   7▼

▲8

8. For the export market, always important to all helicopter manufacturers, Bell has developed the Model 406 Combat Scout with the new four-bladed main rotor system from the OH-58D and armed with light support weapons such as those shown here: the two-unit 7.62mm machine-gun pod and the 18–round 70mm rocket launcher for fin-folding aerial rockets such as the new Hydra 70 series. The long nose probe is purely for flight test purposes. This helicopter could be purchased by Jordan, Saudi Arabia or Pakistan. (Bell)

9. Going one step further, the Bell TexasRanger is a development of the Model 206, armed with missiles for a light attack/armed reconnaissance role. This example has been used by Emerson Electronics to test the Hughes Aircraft TOW in the Emerson/Saab HeliTOW arrangement which has been acquired by the Swedish Army for the BO 105C helicopter. Note the TOW launchers on the fuselage racks and the large HeliTOW sight above the cabin. (Emerson)

▼9

10. Two examples from the newly acquired Rogerson-Hiller Company, using an old design much developed for future low-intensity battlefield needs. On the right is the RH-1100 (the successor to the 1961 vintage OH-5) which is unarmed, and to the left is the new RH-1100M Hornet. The Hornet is credited with the scout, armed reconnaissance, observation and attack roles, all in one airframe, thus providing smaller countries with a very cost-effective helicopter package. Note the Hornet 6's nose-mounted M65 TOW missile sight. (Rogerson)

11. The British Army, although not slow to enter the helicopter business, was restricted in its use of armed helicopters for many years. The Westland Scout has performed several functions within the Army Air Corps, including scout, observation, armed patrol insertion and, later, anti-tank helicopter duties. This example of a Scout AH 1 is from 651 Squadron AAC and is demonstrating the deployment of armed troops for forward patrol purposes. (Author's collection)

▲12   ▼13

12. A nation which has been continually at war since 1962 is the Republic of South Africa, where the helicopter force is almost entirely French in origin. The Alouette III (seen here near Table Mountain, Cape Town) has been used for a variety of tasks including armed reconnaissance and troop insertion. Because of the difficult sand-filled atmosphere in southern Africa, operational Alouette are fitted with 'elephant ears' sand filters. (Author's collection)

13. An early but highly successful attempt to arm helicopters was made by the Rhodesian Air Force, during the 1972–79 bush war, when its K-cars were fitted with a variety of weapons from the 12.7mm Browning to the 20mm cannon seen here on an Alouette III. Note the cutaway cabin flooring which allows the gun to be trained downwards. During fire fights, the armed Alouette III would support the ground troops of the Rhodesian Light Infantry by providing very effective fire. It is thought that the Air Force of Zimbabwe has used the same techniques to support government troops in Mozambique. (Author's collection)

14. For advanced reconnaissance and to support the anti-tank teams of Lynx helicopters, the British Army is equipped with more than 100 SA 341 Gazelle helicopters. At present unarmed, the Gazelle AH 1 (which also serves with the 3rd Commando Brigade Air Squadron, Royal Marines) has recently been equipped with the Ferranti AF 532 observation aid (seen above the cockpit) and the Racal Mini-TANS tactical air navigation system. Trials to equip Gazelle with the Shorts Javelin proved the systems to be incompatible and the Starstreak development is awaited to provide self-defence for the Gazelle and the Lynx teams. (Ferranti)

15. Besides the British-made sight, the French manufacturer SFIM also markets a Gazelle roof-compatible observation aid, based on the highly successful APX M397 HOT anti-tank missile system aiming sight which is fitted to the French ALAT (Army Light Aviation) Gazelle and the German Heeresflieger (Army Aviation) BO 105P helicopters. Note the sight controller (lower left) and the visor (centre) with the observation aid itself on the cabin roof. (SFIM)

16. To accommodate the Ferranti observation aid, the Gazelle's cockpit roof had to be remodelled. The sight – known as GOA or Gazelle Observation Aid to the Army Air Corps – is shown in its self-stow position. (Author's collection)

14▲

15▲   16▼

▲17   ▼18

17. During the Falklands campaign, British Gazelle were armed with MATRA SNEB rocket pods, capable of taking 70mm unguided rockets for ground fire suppression and possible use against enemy aircraft. In the event, the Gazelle pilots did not use the weapons, but the positive effect on aircrew morale has resulted in the writing of a staff requirement for some form of self-defence system for the Gazelle. This Gazelle AH 1 served with the Royal Marines and is being re-armed ashore prior to a sortie. (British Army photograph)

18. In France, several attempts have been made to arm the Gazelle for armed reconnaissance and close-support operations, including the fitting of the Giat M621 20mm cannon system. The starboard side mounting is capable of being trained in elevation, but fires directly down the axis of the helicopter, being aimed by the pilot. Developments include the use of a second port-side configured cannon, but it is more usual to balance the mounting with that of the 70mm Brandt or Forges Zeebrugges rocket launcher. (Author's collection)

19. A close-up of the Giat M621 20mm cannon mounting on the Gazelle SA 342M light armed reconnaissance helicopter, showing the weapons' cross-beam and ammunition feed from the rear cabin. This configuration has been exported to several African nations including Gabon. (Giat)

20. Crouzet's helicopter sighting system for light helicopters armed with guns, rockets or light anti-tank missiles is seen here on a development Gazelle. One version of the French-made system can be optimized for the air-to-air self-defence deployment of missiles, as well as for the more conventional gun and rocket roles. The sight has been cleared for operation from Gazelle, Ecureuil, Dauphin, Panther and Puma helicopters. (Crouzet)

19▲ 20▼

21. First flown in 1985, the Aérospatiale AS 350L1 Ecureuil helicopter is attracting attention from the developing nations and has been sold in Africa (Swaziland, Malawi and Botswana). Photographed at the Mediterranean weapons range near Toulon, the AS 350L1 development helicopter shown here is fitted with the M621 20mm cannon and has provision for 70mm rocket launchers on the port weapons beam. (Aérospatiale)

22. Not strictly an armed helicopter, the AS 350L1 shows its ability to operate with a ground-based Milan anti-tank missile team in a battlefield environment. Originally designed as an Alouette III replacement, the Ecureuil (Squirrel) has proved successful during trials, but is restricted to low-intensity conflicts or indirect attention because of its structure and configuration. (Aérospatiale)

▲21   ▼22

23. The twin-engined Ecureuil 2 or Twin Squirrel has recently entered the battlefield helicopter market, having been acquired by the French Air Force, and is now being offered in an armed reconnaissance or light attack role with the standard 20mm cannon and 70mm rocket launcher configuration. (Aérospatiale)

24. With a maximum take-off weight of 2.5 tonnes, the AS 355M2 Ecureuil 2 is aimed at an increasing market of patrol, counter-insurgency, protection and light attack. In many ways this is the more traditional role of the armed helicopter as it is only recently that large numbers of larger, more powerful attack helicopters have been produced by the two Super Powers. (Aérospatiale)

25. Designed to fulfil a civilian role, the Agusta A109 has recently been under development with the Turboméca Arriel engine to provide better high and hot performance required in so many Middle Eastern and African theatres. Armed with machine-gun and rocket pods, the A109K has yet to be ordered, but the manufacturer is confident of an important market share over the next few years. (Agusta)

26. Appealing to several South and Central American nations, some of which have purchased the helicopter, the McDonnell Douglas Nightfox is a development of the successful 500MD Defender attack helicopter. The Nightfox has been optimized for night operations, using the FLIR (forward-looking infra-red) system (under chin) and being armed with two 7.62mm machine-guns. (McDonnell Douglas)

Early Development
of the Attack Helicopter

Having seen the need of helicopter-borne air power during the disastrous war in Indo-China, the French forces set about developing armament systems for their helicopters operating in the Algerian War of Independence. It soon became clear to a number of nations that there was a need of lightly armed helicopters in the post-colonial wars; the US Army began its weapon equipments with the Bell H-13 Sioux and later developed very effective mountings for the Bell UH-1 Huey which entered service in 1958.

In 1961, Bell Helicopter delivered the first 'gunship' version of the HU-1B (later UH-1B) to the US Army. This helicopter was armed with a flexi-mount 12.7mm machine-gun and a 40mm grenade launcher. Both these weapons were to be used effectively throughout the Vietnam War, including installations on other UH-1 types and on the AH-1 Cobra which entered service in 1967. During 1963–4 (with the US Army's Tactical Mobility Requirements Board having issued a staff requirement for an armed helicopter the year before), Bell demonstrated the Sioux Scout test-bed, based on the H-13 observation helicopter, which formed the basis for the later Model 209 Cobra. The Sioux Scout featured a tandem-seat layout and twin 7.62mm machine-guns mounted in the helicopter's nose. The dedicated attack helicopter stems directly from the Sioux Scout and has passed through the armed utility type, to the dedicated attack helicopter (1967) and on to the advanced attack helicopter (1986); the current forecast is for the next step to be the LHX (Light Helicopter Experiment) SCAT (SCout ATtack) helicopter (1995), and the eventual progression could be to the tilt-rotor, advancing blade or X-wing air vehicle of the next century.

In Europe, all four major helicopter manufacturing nations – Britain, France, Italy and Federal Germany – together with the Dutch aerospace industry have considered dedicated attack helicopters at various times, but the first armed helicopters were developed in the American pattern by using utility helicopters with add-on weapons systems.

In the United Kingdom, the Westland Scout, which was designed as a liaison, scout and observation helicopter to replace the Skeeter, was developed to carry the French Nord SS.11 wire-guided missile system using a roof-mounted Ferranti direct view optical sight. The helicopter served in British Army of the Rhine in this guise and was also deployed to the Falklands in 1982 with the missile system, but in the absence of enemy armoured vehicles, the missile flight was used to destroy reinforced ground positions, such as bunkers. In this anti-tank role, the Scout's performance was limited, but the basic operational philosophies were developed, leading to the Lynx/TOW combination and eventually it is hoped to the Light Attack Helicopter (LAH) programme, currently based around the A129 Tonal project.

Early French attack helicopter trials included the fitting of the SS.1's predecessor, the SS.10, to the Sud-Ouest Djinn, a turbogenerator-propelled helicopter which was tested by American, French and Federal German forces in the early and mid 1950s. The helicopter did not enter operational service with the missile armament, presumably because the airframe/powerplant combination was not considered effective. Sud-Est, another small French design house which amalgamated with Sud-Ouest in 1957 (to form Sud Aviation) and in 1970 with Nord to form Aérospatiale, was engaged in the Alouette II programme. This light helicopter, still in service with the British Army and other forces, was armed with the SS.11, but its larger brother, the Alouette III, was found to be a better and more effective mount.

The Alouette III has been variously equipped with the Nord SS.11 and AS.12 wire-guided missile, and the French ALAT only recently disbanded its anti-tank flights equipped with the combination, replacing them with the Gazelle/HOT anti-tank system. The Alouette III is a robust, stable launch platform, hence its longevity as a battlefield helicopter, having served with distinction in conflicts in Angola, SWA/Namibia, Mozambique, Rhodesia and South Africa.

Following the NATO powers, the Soviet Union decided that the quickest way to bring an attack helicopter into service was to use add-on weapons such as the 57mm rocket launchers of the fixed-wing forces and a development of various ground-based wire-guided and radio-controlled anti-tank missiles. The helicopter chosen was the medium weight Mi-8 (Hip) rather than the smaller, possibly more agile Mi-2 (Hoplite), although this helicopter too has been armed. The Mi-8 Hip-E (the true Soviet definition has not been released) can carry a very large range of ordnance, including free-fall bombs, rockets, anti-tank missiles and guns; all the armament has been tested in Afghanistan.

The success of the Mi-8 and the possible threat from the People's Republic of China in the late 1960s, led to the development of the Mi-24 (Hind) assault helicopter; this development is dealt with separately.

From the above, it can be seen that the original attack helicopter concepts were based on the light, observation and scout helicopters in the West, while the Soviets used the larger, longer endurance transport types. This is not surprising when one considers the terrain of the USSR from the East German and Polish borders to the Urals where helicopter training takes place – it is flat countryside with no place for the helicopter to wait in ambush and therefore it is ideal territory for the heavy assault-type attack helicopter.

27. Dipping low across the Mekong Delta, this US Navy Bell UH-1B Huey gunship shows off its rocket and machine-gun war load during US operations in Vietnam, *circa* 1968. These Hueys were based ashore and afloat, being used to provide fire support for assault, rescue and reconnaissance operations by other US and Vietnamese forces. The arming of the basic utility Huey paved the way for the dedicated attack helicopter. (Bell)

28. Also operational with America's Australian allies, the Huey, seen here in its larger, more powerful version (UH-1H Huey), carrying rocket launchers and mini-guns during a training sortie in 1983. Nearly twenty years after the Royal Australian Air Force operated from Vung Tau, the Australian forces have yet to receive anything more powerful than the Huey gunship for army co-operation, fire support and direct fire roles. Seen here, a typical air lift of trooping helicopters, escorted by the armed Huey (right). The helicopters are from 9 Squadron, RAAF. (RAAF/Mal Lancaster)

27▲ 28▼

29. The arrival of the Bell Cobra changed the pattern of US Army helicopter operations in Vietnam, for now the aviation effort included a dedicated attack helicopter armed with the trainable undernose gun turret and 70mm rockets. Note that this AH-1G Cobra is also armed with a stub-wing mounted rotating mini-gun besides the rockets, nose 7.62mm and grenade launcher. (Bell)

30. Impressed by the success of the US Army with the dedicated attack helicopter, the US Marine Corps organized a requirement for its own version, but with two engines for overwater flight safety. This example, seen on a test flight from Bell's Fort Worth (Texas) facility,

▲29   ▼30

is armed with four 70mm rocket launchers and what appears to be a sensor probe for a test flight data collection where the 20mm cannon would normally fit. The AH-1J retains the two-bladed wide-chord main rotor system. (Bell)

31. Being of clean lines, narrow head-on perspective and relatively well powered, the Cobra family has been taken as a model for future attack helicopter designs. The helicopter is still in production nearly 20 years after the first prototype was flown. The first twin-engine version, the AH-1J, also supplied to Iran and Spain, is still in US Marine Corps service with the USMC Reserve. (Author's collection)

31▲

32. Somehow the Scout does not look as ungainly as other utility/scout helicopters which have been converted to accommodate add-on anti-tank missiles to provide an interim attack helicopter configuration. In this early view of the Scout/SS.11 combination, a development aircraft is shown operating over Salisbury Plain. The four missiles are shown on outrigger launchers, two to each side of the helicopter's fuselage. The SS.11 is controlled by the aircrewman/gunner seated in the left-hand seat, operating the Ferranti roof-mounted sight, with guidance provided by wires projecting from each missile in flight. (Museum of Army Flying)

33. The attack helicopter is not a weapon for autonomous use, and in the same way that infantry and tanks have to be supported, it operates to maximum advantage with other direct fire arms. After the French Army's experience in Indo-China and Algeria, the combined arms technique of armed helicopters supporting infantry and tanks was developed with the Alouette III/SS.11 combination. In real operations, the helicopter would not be so vulnerable, exposed above the attacking infantry. (Aérospatiale)

▲32 ▼33

American Attack Helicopters

A major pioneer of the helicopter on the battlefield, the US Army became the world's third largest 'air force' in 1970 during the Vietnam and other South-East Asian conflicts. It is credited with the deployment of the first dedicated attack helicopter – the AH-1G Cobra – the subsequent development of the type into a guided missile firing weapon system for anti-tank operations and the deployment of the first true advanced attack helicopter, the AH-64A Apache.

The American helicopter industry has also developed a number of light attack helicopters which although not procured in any numbers by the US Army or US Marine Corps have nevertheless been extremely successful around the world. According to well-placed US sources, the 500MD has been purchased by the US military for special operations, and examples were seen on TV during the invasion of Grenada in 1983.

Using the Allison 250 turboshaft engine, Hughes Helicopters (now McDonnell Douglas Helicopter Company) developed the observation OH-6A into the Model 500MD Defender as a lightweight attack helicopter capable of mounting guns, rockets or missiles for day-only anti-tank and close support operations, primarily in Third World nations. The Defender is manufactured under licence in South Korea (Korean Airlines) and Italy (Breda-Nardi, a subsidiary of Agusta). The Defender has seen action in Kenya during a *coup d'état* and in Lebanon when Israeli forces used the helicopter against Syrian tank formations with a success rate of 15 : 1. It is also possible that the helicopter has been in action in Central and South America.

Rogerson-Hiller, the phoenix of the former Hiller Company, has recently commenced marketing the RH-1100M Hornet which is a missile-armed development of the Fairchild-Hiller FH-1100 executive helicopter. The Hornet should appeal to the world's smaller nations who need a powerful helicopter yet cannot afford a modern battlefield type with the high-priced survivability measures of say, the Cobra.

The Cobra is an American success story. The design was re-evaluated by the US Army in August 1965 and the first order was received by Texas-based Bell Helicopter in April 1966. A year later the first helicopters were in action in Vietnam, the first six arriving for the New Equipment Training Team in September 1967, the peak year of American effort in that country. Well armoured, tandem-seated and fast, the Cobra could engage enemy positions and survive, as well as provide escort to the troop-carrying UH-1 Huey. Initially, the helicopters were armed with machine-guns, cannon and rockets, with wire-guided missiles only coming in the later stages of the war.

According to the official war history, the Cobra was responsible for the relief of Bien Hoa Air Base which, had it not been for four Cobra gunships, would have been overrun by the Vietcong. There were many other such incidents.

In the European theatre, however, the Cobra would require the Hughes Aircraft M65 chin-mounted sight and the TOW anti-tank missile system to pose an effective deterrent to the Warsaw Pact's overwhelming tank forces coming across the Inner German Border. Initially, 93 AH-1Q Cobra were prepared at Bell from AH-1G airframes, and later several hundred were given uprated engines to bring them to AH-1S standard. Until about 1983, the Cobra was the only dedicated attack helicopter in production in the Western world and the US Army acquired some 1,800 AH-1G/S models, including the Enhanced Cobra and the Modernized S model with aircraft survivability systems such as infra-red jammers, laser range finders and the GEC Avionics air data system for added information input when the helicopter is hovering for missile firing.

The AH-1S's armament suite includes the provision of a 20mm gun turret, and weapons stations on the stud wing for 70mm rockets and TOW missiles. The canopy has been re-designed to a low glint, angular shape, and extra armour has been fitted to the tandem crew compartment, where the gunner sits in the front and the pilot in the rear.

The US Marine Corps, impressed with the AH-1G in Vietnam, took delivery of a few for trials before acquiring the twin-engined AH-1J SeaCobra in the early 1970s. For shipborne operations, twin engine safety is most important and gives better performance in hot and high conditions. The International version of the AH-1J was sold to Spain and Iran, where the helicopter has been seen in combat with Soviet and American-built Iraqi equipment.

The AH-1G/Q/S series has also been exported, and in mid 1986 was still in production for Jordan, Pakistan, Greece and Turkey. Surprisingly, despite the helicopter's successful service with USAREUR (US Army in Europe), the Federal German forces decided against the type as the PAH-2, even when offered with four-bladed main rotor and Euromissile HOT night firing capability. Federal Germany decided to proceed with the Eurocopter PAH-2 project after the Apache had been decided against at the highest political level.

The US Marine Corps has continued a policy of updating its SeaCobra force to the AH-1T SeaCobra (with new production and retrofitting) and in 1986 with the introduction of the AH-1W (formerly AH-1T+) SuperCobra helicopter, powered by a similar variant of the Apache's General Electric T700 engines. It is possible that all remaining SeaCobra will be enhanced to the AH-1W level during the next five to ten years.

Initially, Bell entered the KingCobra variant, the YAH-63, for the US Army's Advanced Attack Helicopter competition (which replaced the Advanced Aerial Fire Support System competition of 1965) and faced stiff competition from Hughes Helicopters with the YAH-64. Both helicopters were required to carry the same armament of 30mm cannon and 16 Hellfire missiles, be powered by the General Electric T700 engine and have night fighting capability. Besides the Hellfire laser-guided missiles, the two helicopters were required to show their abilities with the 70mm unguided fin-folding aerial rocket. Bell's design was two-bladed and the Hughes had four blades.

In December 1976, the US Army decided to proceed with the YAH-64 design which Hughes Helicopters now called the Apache. The Apache is the Western world's first advanced attack helicopter capable of night and adverse weather operations, able to carry laser-guided munitions and with various impressive survivability features such as the ability of the main gearbox to continue safe operation for 30 minutes after the loss of all lubricating oil.

For night flying, especially nap-of-the-earth, the Apache is equipped with the Martin Marietta PNVS or Pilot's Night Vision System which occupies the nose of the helicopter, along with the TADS or Target Acquisition Designation System from the same manufacturer. TADS is equipped with direct view optics, infra-red visionics, TV, a laser designator and a laser rangefinder. Although the Apache is destined to operate with OH-58C Kiowa and later OH-58D Aeroscout helicopters as part of a fire team, the helicopter is capable of operating solo except that it is not provided with any self-defence missiles, such as Stinger (as on the OH-58D) or Sidewinder (on the AH-1W).

The US Army would like to retain 1,000 Cobra and have an additional 675 Apache for such operations as cross-FLOT (forward line of own troops) assaults to penetrate an enemy rear area. The Cobra will be supplemented and then replaced by the LHX-SCAT from 1996/97 onwards.

During the development of the Apache, Hughes Helicopters (now McDonnell Douglas) did not neglect the further development of the 500 series and in 1984 announced the 530MG Defender. The helicopter is especially suited to the low-intensity battlefield where an attack helicopter is required, but where the force involved cannot afford or would not find a dedicated tandem-seat attack helicopter cost-effective. The 530MG has the ability to be used for armed reconnaissance, anti-tank, close support and similar tasks. The basic equipment of the 530MG includes a chin-mounted forward-looking infra-red (FLIR) system, a Hughes Aircraft mast-mounted sight, TOW missiles, McDonnell Douglas 7.62mm chain gun or 70mm rockets.

The most important feature of the helicopter is the mission management and cockpit display systems which have been fully integrated to reduce pilot and co-pilot/gunner workloads, while operating nap-of-the-earth or in hostile terrain. Basically the pilot is given only the data required for a particular flight manoeuvre, but in the event of an emergency other critical information is digitally displayed. The CRTs (TV screens) used will also display the view from the FLIR and the TV camera in the mast-mounted sight. The mission management system is produced by the British Racal Avionics group, and the joint development of the 530MG Defender has been a major triumph for Anglo-American co-operation. Other nations involved include Belgium with BARCO SA developing the display units and FN Herstal developing the special gun and rocket pods.

The 530MG has been sold to several Central and South American customers, but for local security reasons details are very vague. Some other nations in that part of the world have also been interested in the 500/530 Nightfox combination which uses a non-military standard (therefore cheaper) FLIR and a combination of guns and rockets to give a multi-role security and border protection helicopter.

The Nightfox was shown for the first time at the Asian Aerospace Show at Singapore in January 1986 and is in the middle of the current McDonnell Douglas 500 series range which in ascending order consists of the 500 Paramilitary, 500 Scout, Nightfox, 500/530MG/TOW and the top of the range 500/530MG MMS/TOW with the integrated cockpit. The Nightfox is specially designed to give day or night operation and should attract considerable attention worldwide.

Although generally known for light, medium and heavy transport helicopter models which it has produced over the years – names like Choctaw, Black Hawk, Sea Stallion and Super Stallion – Sikorsky Aircraft has also been closely associated with light attack helicopters during the past few years, leading to the development of the AUH-76 version of the successful S-76 offshore transport and executive helicopter. In fact, the AUH-76 can claim to have played an important and substantial part in the resignation of President Marcos from power in The Philippines when the attack squadron which flew the helicopter defected to the 'rebel' side and supported the newly elected President Aquino.

Not satisfied with the AUH-76's performance, Sikorsky used the Pratt & Whitney of Canada PT6 powerplant to develop the H-76 Eagle multi-role helicopter which is capable of undertaking roles from that of TOW-armed attack helicopter to troop assault transport, medical evacuation helicopter or load lifter. The Eagle's market is non-US military, except perhaps for a few special operations type tasks, but there is an important market in the world for a capable helicopter which can be utilized in several roles during a day on the battlefield.

Although the AUH-76 has been sold in South-East Asia and the Pacific, the Eagle has yet (mid 1986) to receive an order, but it is considered a favourite for several competitions in the Middle and Far East.

The North American helicopter industry has produced a wide range of attack helicopters in recent years – from the extremely capable Apache and Cobra series to the light, multi-role types such as the Eagle, Defender and Hornet. It is still a strong industry despite recession and it should continue to have a substantial market internationally, despite growing technological expertize from Europe and several other areas.

AMERICAN-DESIGNED ATTACK HELICOPTERS

Manufacturer	**Bell**
Model	**AH-1S Modernized Cobra**
Service entry	1982
Engines	1 × Lycoming T53-L-703
Crew	2
Gross weight	4535kg (10000lb)
Max speed	170 knots (315km/h)
Range	317nm (587km)
Weapons	1 × 20mm cannon; 8 × TOW anti-tank missiles or 70mm rocket launchers

Manufacturer	**Bell**
Model	**AH-1W SuperCobra**
Service entry	1986
Engines	2 × General Electric T700-GE-401
Crew	2
Gross weight	6691kg (14750lb)
Max speed	165 knots (306km/h)
Range	300nm (556km)
Weapons	1 × 20mm cannon; 8 × TOW-2/Hellfire anti-tank missiles; Sidewinder, Sidearm or Stinger air-to-air missiles; 70mm rocket launchers

Manufacturer	**Bell**
Model	**206 TexasRanger**
Service entry	1983
Engines	1 × Allison 250-C30P
Crew	2
Gross weight	1950kg (4300lb)
Max speed	122 knots (226km/h)
Range	330nm (611km)
Weapons	4 × TOW anti-tank missiles; 2 × 70mm rocket launchers; 7.62mm/ 12.7mm gun pods

Manufacturer	**McDonnell Douglas Helicopters**
Model	**530 MG**
Service entry	1986
Engines	1 × Allison 250-C30B
Crew	2
Gross weight	1361kg (3000lb)
Max speed	122 knots (226km/h)
Range	203nm (376km)
Weapons	4 × TOW anti-tank missiles; 7.62mm or 12.7mm gun pods; 70mm rocket launchers

Manufacturer	**McDonnell Douglas Helicopters**
Model	**AH-64A Apache**
Service entry	1986
Engines	2 × General Electric T700-GE-701
Crew	2
Gross weight	9318kg (20500lb)
Max speed	197 knots (365km/h)
Range	330nm (611km)
Weapons	1 × 30mm chain gun; 16 × Hellfire anti-tank missiles; 4 × 70mm rocket launchers

Manufacturer	**Rogerson-Hiller**
Model	**RH-1100M Hornet**
Service entry	(awaiting orders)
Engines	1 × Allison 250-C20B
Crew	2
Gross weight	1406kg (3100lb)
Max speed	110 knots (204km/h)
Range	534nm (990km)
Weapons	4 × TOW anti-tank missiles; 7.62mm or 12.7mm gun pods; 70mm rocket launchers

Manufacturer	**Sikorsky**
Model	**H-76 Eagle**
Service entry	(awaiting orders)
Engines	2 × Pratt & Whitney PT6B-36
Crew	2
Gross weight	4989kg (11000lb)
Max speed	155 knots (287km/h)
Range	353nm (654km)
Weapons	16 × TOW anti-tank missiles; 70mm rocket launchers; 7.62mm or 12.7mm gun pods

34. In the mid 1980s, the US Army carried out a number of trials to develop tactics and equipment requirements for a light armed reconnaissance helicopter to support the advanced attack helicopter fleet. Included in the trials was the Bell OH-58J Kiowa, equipped with the SFENA Ministab stability augmentation system, target sight and weapons guidance head-up display for rocket delivery.

35. At Fort Lewis, Washington State, the 9th Infantry Division experimented with various helicopter configurations, including the OH-58C Kiowa armed with TOW, rockets and gun pods. Note the low profile skids and the folding main blades for air transportation as part of a rapid reaction force. (US Army)

36. Firing a TOW anti-tank missile, this is the development Bell 206L TexasRanger helicopter, developed from the LongRanger corporate helicopter, itself developed from the Kiowa/JetRanger series. (Bell)

37. Firing the Emerson-Saab HeliTOW missile during tests in the United States. The development 406CS is proving the concept already in service with the MBB BO 105C of the Swedish armed forces. The TOW missile is wire-guided. (Emerson)

38. Called the Model 412 Armed Helicopter by the manufacturers, Bell Helicopter Textron, this helicopter carries the British-built Lucas 12.7mm gun turret under the nose. Its purpose is to provide light attack capability in a troop-lifting helicopter. (Bell)

▲34 ▼35

36▲

37▲   38▼

◄39,40,41. A sequence of photographs showing a McDonnell Douglas (Hughes) 500MD Defender, equipped with a mast-mounted sight, firing a TOW missile during tests to prove the Hughes Aircraft Company's fire control system via the mast-mounted sight. The MMS gives the helicopter's crew the tactical flexibility to hide behind trees, buildings or natural features, and to remain out of sight and therefore protected from enemy defensive action.

42. Mocked-up for a feature film, this Bell 222A really belongs to Air Hanson, a British-based executive helicopter operator. Several films and TV shows have recently shown the use of attack helicopters of unrealistic capabilities, such as the 'Mach 1' AirWolf and Blue Thunder.

43. A close-up of the 500MD Defender's cockpit and lightweight TOW missile launchers. Above the rotor blades, are the TV lenses of the mast-mounted sight, which has room for a thermal-imaging module to be fitted. Note that the pilot-in-command flies the 500MD from the right-hand seat (unlike other conventional side-by-side helicopters) with the co-pilot/gunner in the left seat.

42▲   43▼

44. Once in the air, the 500MD is an agile and adaptable light attack helicopter. In this view the two twin TOW launchers and the characteristic T-tail of the design are shown. The helicopter carries a US civil registration and the word 'experimental' for missile firing trials and customer demonstrations.

45. Out on the range in US Marine Corps base, Camp Pendleton in California, the 500MD launches a TOW missile against a target some 4,000m (2.5 miles) away for the benefit of European military attachés. The MMS version of the Defender, based on the 500D airframe, did not sell to overseas nations, but it is possible that some were purchased by the US Army's Special Operations Task Force.

▲44   ▼45

46. A 500MD Defender, armed with the TOW missile system, as operated by the 50th Air Cavalry of the Kenyan Army immediately prior to the coup attempt in 1982. Supported by the US Army's systems command and others, the Kenyan forces soon learned how to operate the Defender with its Hughes Aircraft M65 chin-mounted sight. It is possible that some of the Kenyan Defenders were used against rebels during the coup attempt.

47. The small profile of the Defender is a clear advantage during attack operations, when such techniques as nap-of-the-earth flying (keeping close to the ground and not exposing the helicopter above feature lines) improve the helicopter's tactical advantage on the battlefield.

46▲   47▼

▲48　▼49

48. The most successful operator of the Defender in warfare has been the Israeli Defence Force which used the helicopters, again armed with the TOW missile, against targets in the Bekaa Valley in Lebanon during the Israeli invasion of 1982, code-named 'Peace in Galilee'. It is reported that the Defenders destroyed 15 tanks and armoured vehicles for every one of their own number lost; some were lost because Israel ordered another batch of the helicopters from the then Hughes Helicopters, which since 1985 has been called the McDonnell Douglas Helicopter Company.

49. Other export customers for the 500MD include Colombia, South Korea and Taiwan; between 1982–84, a number of civilian 500 were exported to North Korea and may have been configured to military standards, but it is not thought that they are able to carry missiles. Seen here are the TOW launcher (port) and 7.62mm pod machine-gun combination for a light attack role.

50. By 1983, the 500MD MMS Defender was being superseded by a developed model of the airframe, but there is no doubt that the experience gained with the mast-mounted sight, TOW missiles and agile airframe have contributed to the bid which McDonnell Douglas is making, with Bell Helicopter Textron, for the US Army's futuristic LHX programme.

51. Destined to enter production in 1987, but not to serve with the US Army, the Rogerson-Hiller RH 1100M Hornet is a development of the piston-engined Hiller 1100, but has the Allison 250 engine and is armed with TOW missiles. The aim of the helicopter is to provide a cost-effective light attack capability to small nations wishing to protect their borders and fixed installations against small, well-armed groups. The Hornet is equipped with the HAC M65 chin-mounted sight.

▲ 52

▲ 53   ▼ 54

52. Developed for the Vietnam War, the Bell AH-1G Cobra was the first successful tandem-seated attack helicopter and has served as a bench-mark for the other designs which have followed in North America and Europe. The original G model was only fitted for guns (like the 20mm chin-turret) and rockets on the stub-wing pylons. Simple and rugged, the Cobra achieved fame in the Mekong Delta and other locations; almost all the existing US Army, reserve and army national guard operators had received the updated S model Cobra by early 1987.

53. Early tests with the Hughes Aircraft Company's Tube-launched Optically-tracked, Wire-guided (TOW) missile, known to the US Army as the AGM-71, were carried out with the Cobra in the late 1960s, and in June 1975 the first AH-1Q entered service. However, it was found that carrying TOW required more power to compensate for weight and the Modified S model (illustrated) was born.

54. Three types of TOW missile shown at one of the annual US Army Aviation conferences: (bottom) TOW, (middle) I-TOW or Improved TOW and (upper) TOW-2. Most US Army units have now received TOW-2, while other NATO partners, including the British Army, have I-TOW, but this will be further modified with top-attack fuzes by 1988. The TOW missile should continue in effective service until 2000. (Author's collection)

55. A number of AH-1G/Q Cobra were modified to S standard by Bell in the mid to late 1970s, such as this helicopter which serves with the Army National Guard in Texas. Early USAREUR (US Army in Europe) Cobra were updated using kits supplied to Dornier, the German aircraft manufacturer in Bavaria.

56. The major modifications for the S model Cobra are in powerplant, avionics and systems, as well as the more angular cockpit transparencies which are said to prevent sun glint giving away the helicopter's position when waiting to ambush armoured vehicles. In this view of the AH-1S Cobra, note the TOW missile tubes, chin-mounted sight and thin cross-section of the helicopter.

57. Members of the élite 82nd Airborne Division supervise the unloading of an AH-1S from a USAF C-5A Galaxy transport during one of the joint US-Egyptian reinforcement exercises in the 'Bright Star' series. In the Galaxy, the Cobra does not need to be substantially broken down and can be readied for action within minutes of arriving at an overseas location. The Cobra was used by the Rapid Deployment Joint Task Force as an escort helicopter for trooping, as well as for attack tasks.

58. There are about 1,000 Cobra currently in service with the US Army, and most of those are in USAREUR (US Army Europe), operating with the NATO forces close to the Inner German Border. This AH-1S is undertaking a regular patrol on the border between Federal Germany and Czechoslovakia where in the past Cobra have been engaged by Warsaw Pact aircraft. Note the snake motif on the rotor housing. (W W Duck)

59. The final US Army Cobra S model is fitted with the GEC Avionics air data sensor (above the co-pilot/gunner's cockpit) and various electronic warfare equipment for battlefield survivability. Note the exhaust efflux cooler, the Sanders IR-missile jammer and the Perkin-Elmer laser warning system above the rear cockpit. The helicopter is painted in the new hot/high grey colour for non-European operations. (Perkin-Elmer)

60. A close-up of the Perkin-Elmer AN/AVR-2 laser warning system (right), the Sanders AN/ALQ-144 (variant) countermeasures system (centre left) and the exhaust shroud. In the bottom right are two TOW launcher tail pipes. (Perkin-Elmer)

58▲

59▲   60▼

61. Flying in formation on a pre-delivery test flight, two of the 40 or so AH-1S Cobra of various types which have been supplied to the Israeli Defence Force. Note that the pilots are alone, in the rear seat, and that no national markings have been applied to the light olive-drab paint scheme. Cobra acquitted themselves well during the 1982 invasion of Lebanon. (Bell)

62. An example of the AH-1S as delivered from Bell's Fort Worth (Texas) plant. The helicopter is armed with the 20mm 3-barrelled Gatling-type gun in the nose turret and eight TOW missile launchers (only one round is in place in this picture). Operating with the Kiowa and later the Aeroscout helicopters of an Air Cavalry attack team, the Cobra is a powerful attack helicopter and a major anti-tank asset in the NATO inventory. (Bell)

61▼   62▲

▲63　　▼64

63. Flying near Mount Fuji in Japan, one of the first AH-1S Cobra to be delivered to the Japanese Ground Self-Defence Force. Japanese Cobra are armed with TOW missiles co-produced under licence for Hughes Aircraft by Nippon Electric Company Ltd. Japanese tactics call for the missiles to be used against small ships as well as tanks. (HAC)

64. During training exercises, the first two Fuji-buit Cobra undertake a dawn patrol along a river bed. With deliveries in 1982–85, Japan now has a powerful force of about over 70 Cobra, all armed with TOW and rocket launchers, as well as the standard gun. (Fuji)

65. The first Japanese Cobra fires 70mm rockets during in-country trials of the weapons system. Although a relatively small nation, Japan is concerned about amphibious assaults on its long coastline and sees the flexibility of the attack helicopter as a good way of preventing an enemy from establishing a bridgehead ashore. (Bell)

66. Developed for a European competition to find a new attack helicopter for the Federal German Army, the Model 249 Cobra was the YAH-1 prototype with the four-bladed main rotor system developed for the Bell 412 transport helicopter. It did not succeed in winning any orders, but it was a useful development tool for the later twin-engined US Marine Corps versions.

65▲   66▼

▲67 ▼68

67. After the success of the single-engined AH-1G Cobra in Vietnam, the US Marine Corps ordered a twin-engined version for service ashore and afloat. The AH-1J SeaCobra is powered by the Pratt & Whitney PT6 TwinPac, but carries the same armament as the US Army's AH-1G.

68. Training helicopter pilots to use the flight deck of amphibious assault carriers and other US Navy ships is vital for the US Marines' worldwide role in support of US foreign policy. This unarmed AH-1T SeaCobra is being unlashed prior to launch. (Bell)

69. In Grenada, during the 1983 invasion by US forces, the AH-1T provided tremendous air support from only four helicopters initially employed. Note the additional countermeasures equipment on this helicopter, including the Sanders IR jammer and pylon-attached chaff and flare launchers. The helicopter is configured for light attack duties with two TOW missiles on the outboard pylon and a 7-rocket launcher inboard.

70. Departing from an LPA during the Lebanon crisis, a US Marine Corps AH-1T SeaCobra demonstrates its ability to fly from almost any location in support of ground and naval forces. SeaCobra were not used operationally in Lebanon, but proved of great deterrent value.

▲71

71. One of the USMC international roles is to operate in support of NATO forces in Northern Norway, where this AH-1J SeaCobra was photographed in 1983. The SeaCobra provide badly needed attack helicopter support because the Norwegians have no such capability. (Author's collection)

72. Based at Atlanta NAS (Georgia), the last unit still flying the AH-1J is the US Marine Corps Reserve. This helicopter is being readied for a Sunday morning's launch for a training exercise with ground troops. Note that the 20mm cannon is not fitted to the chin turret. (Author's collection)

73. Bell designed a follow-up to the AH-1T which was originally given the AH-1T+ prefix and the name SuperCobra. This development prototype is painted black overall with a golden cobra design and wording. Standard equipment includes the IR jammer and chaff/flare launcher; the nose probe is a non-standard research instrument. (Bell)

74. Powered by the General Electric T700 engine, the AH-1T+ became known as the AH-1W in 1986 and is seen here completing the weapons system development with the clearance to fire the 70mm Hydra rocket rounds which are effective against lightly armoured vehicles, trucks or troops. It might be used for self-defence against attacking helicopters and light jets. The helicopter is painted bright-olive overall with red trials markings. (Bell)

75. In the conventional attack role, the AH-1W SuperCobra is armed with the Hughes Aircraft TOW missile and the 20mm cannon. Note the distinctive, large turboshaft engine exhausts of the T700 which are a good recognition feature for the helicopter. The paint scheme is olive-green overall with black markings. (Bell)

▲72   ▼73

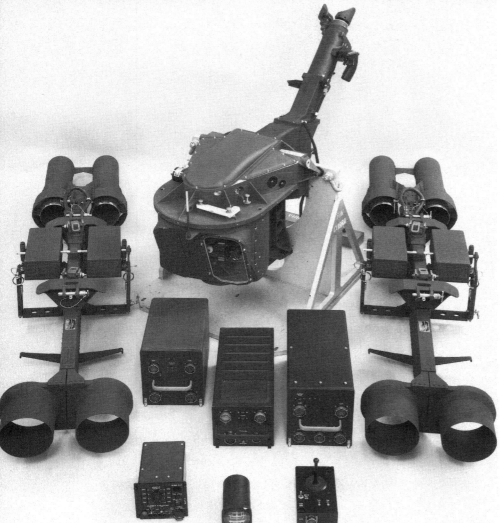

76. The complete air-launched TOW missile system package, including the direct view optical sight (centre), the two TOW launchers (one each side) and the various black boxes for fire control, fire constraints and aiming the missile. (HAC)

77. The Kaiser Electronics head-up display (right) and signal processing equipment for the ground and air firing tasks of the AH-1W.

78. The TOW missile launcher box, fitted to the co-pilot/gunner's cockpit display: here three missiles have been fired and a fourth is armed for manual launch.

79. One of the five YAH-64 advanced attack helicopter prototypes being displayed to British audiences at the 25th Anniversary of the UK's Army Air Corps at Middle Wallop, Hampshire in 1982. Although seeming similar in appearance to the Cobra at first sight, the Apache is larger and better armed. (Beaver/Downey collection)

▲76 ▼77

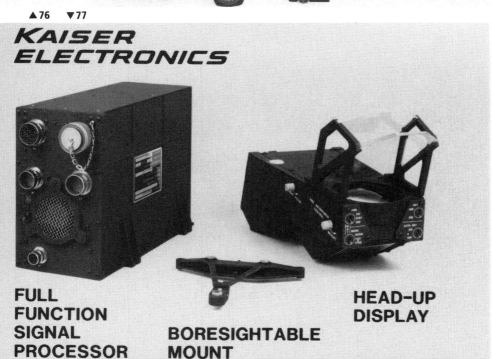

KAISER ELECTRONICS

FULL FUNCTION SIGNAL PROCESSOR

BORESIGHTABLE MOUNT

HEAD-UP DISPLAY

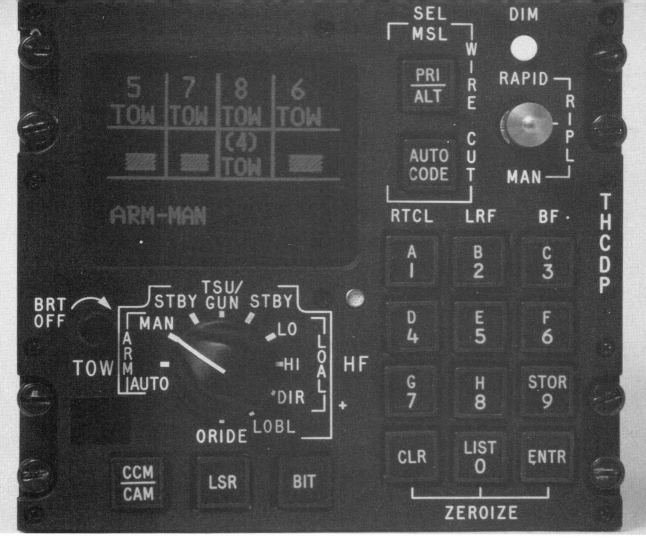

80. Hughes Helicopters (later McDonnell Douglas) won the US Army contract to manage the advanced attack helicopter programme, using the AH-64A Apache as the airframe, fitted with Martin-Marietta's TADS/PNVS (Target Acquisition Data System/Pilot's Night Vision Sensor) and the Rockwell 30mm chain gun. This is an early production model demonstrating its ability to manoeuvre rapidly.

81. During pre-service field trials, the Apache demonstrated its ability despite its greater size compared to previous Western attack helicopters. Note the way in which the Hellfire missiles keep in trim with the ground as the helicopter slows, nose-up, into a firing position.

▲80　▼81

82. The Apache is powered by two General Electric T700 engines which can be reached for maintenance by using the cowling as a work platform, via push-in steps on the side of the fuselage. One of the design features required by the US Army was the ability of the field maintenance teams to work on the helicopter in all conditions with the minimum of gear.

83. A pair of Apache in a field during tests in California. Note the missile racks and the helicopter's size compared to the aircrew standing around. The helicopter's rotor diameter is 48ft (14.63m).

82▲   83▼

84. Rocket firing trials at Camp Pendleton (California). The Apache appears to be in the hover, although one might normally expect it to fly towards the target it is engaging with rockets – it would stand-off heavily defended targets that required anti-tank missiles.

85. The key to the Apache's ability to operate by day and night, even in adverse weather, is the Martin-Marietta TADS/PNVS. The system is split into two independently functioning parts, with the pilot (rear seat) using the PNVS for general flying and the co-pilot/gunner using the TADS to acquire, track and attack a target. Beneath the TADS gimbal is the nose of the 30mm Hughes chain gun developed for the programme. (Martin Marietta)

86. The first operational testing of the Hellfire was undertaken by one of the YAH-64 helicopters. Careful study of the front cockpit will reveal the co-pilot/gunner engrossed in the missile firing operation, using the helicopter's own laser designator for the Hellfire.

85▲   86▼

◄ 87,88,89. A sequence of photographs showing the Hellfire firing sequence from an AH-64A Apache helicopter, after the helicopter had been accepted by the US Army in January 1984, but prior to the first units being formed in April 1986. The first Apache will be flown by the Army National Guard Aviation in September 1987 and the first will arrive for USAREUR service in 1988.

90. The roll-out of the first production Apache at Mesa (Arizona) where McDonnell Douglas has a major facility to build the helicopter and where the various sub-contractors deliver components such as the fuselage, undercarriage, engines, avionics and weaponry. Present for the roll-out in 1983 was a 'real' Apache whose home is also Arizona.

91. In April 1986, the 100th Apache rolled off the line at Mesa for delivery to Fort Hood (Texas) where there are various training units for battalion-scale training and eventual entry into service. In all, the US Army plans to acquire at least 675 Apache for delivery until 1988, with 12 AH-64A being delivered monthly.

90▲   91▼

92. The Apache has been designed to survive in a modern battlefield and still attack enemy targets near or over the forward edge of the battle area. Among the survivability features are armoured but separate cockpits, two separated engine mountings and machinery which is capable of withstanding 23mm explosive shells and continuing to function so that the helicopter can return to base.

93. During the 1982–85 test period, the Apache was flown in many different environments and against various simulated threats. Apparently it came out of the tests with flying colours, but even so there are plans to modify the type with an integrated avionics display cockpit and other modern aids which have been developed in the past five–seven years.

▲92   ▼93

94. Among recent developments is the use of a YAH-64 to demonstrate the LHX (Light Helicopter Experiment) concept; the lighter coloured outline is the size of the planned light attack helicopter of the next century against the size of the present Apache. It is possible that the US Army could eventually specify a modified Apache for the LHX programme. (McDonnell Douglas)

95. Developed from the 500MD Defender, the 530MG version has a completely improved avionics and other systems built into the 500 series airframe. The Hughes Aircraft mast-mounted sight is linked to an undernose forward-looking infra-red system for observation or missile attack profiles. A few 530MG have been sold, but the helicopter may be too advanced for some potential users.

96. Low and fast would be the typical battlefield technique for the 530MG Defender, making it an effectual and cost-effective attack helicopter. It is thought that there is some US Army interest in the helicopter for special operations.

97. Sikorsky is better known for transport helicopters, but in 1983 it developed the offshore oil and executive transport S-76 into an attack helicopter design for Third World countries. The helicopter, now called the AUH-76, can be armed with guns, rockets or missiles and is capable of carrying troops for special operations and supporting them as an attack helicopter. (Sikorsky)

98. Armed with the TOW missile, the AUH-76 can also carry the Hughes mast-mounted sight for observation and missile attack. The type has been used operationally in The Philippines and possibly also in Thailand against Communist insurgents. The Jordanian Air Force flies the helicopter for transport and casualty evacuation tasks. (Sikorsky)

99. Sixteen TOW – the AUH-76 is armed to the teeth. Alternative weapons include cannon, machine-guns (7.62mm and 12.7mm), rockets (Hydra and standard), and the helicopter could be configured for the Franco-German HOT anti-tank missile.

▲96 ▼97

100. During field trials in the United States, the Eagle has shown itself to be a very capable helicopter, especially in the armed reconnaissance and light attack roles, armed with machine-gun or cannon pods. Orders are expected from Middle and Far Eastern nations, as well as South America. (Sikorsky)

101. Displayed for the first time at the 1985 Paris Air Show, the Sikorsky H-76 Eagle is a re-engined and modified version of the AUH-76 which the manufacturer claims is a true multi-role helicopter. It has basically the same weaponry as the AUH, but there is now the possibility of fitting air-to-air guided weapons for self-protection. (J. M. de Casteja)

▲100   ▼101

In its first flight colours, the prototype Lynx-3 multi-role attack helicopter appeared at Middle Wallop Air Day in 1984. Note the wheeled undercarriage. The helicopter is capable of firing Hellfire, TOW or HOT missiles, rockets and various gun and cannon pods. (Author's collection)

The TexasRanger has been developed into the 406 Combat Scout, armed with a variety of weapons, including rockets and 7.62mm gun pods. The helicopter is being shown to various potential buyers for light attack duties, including the armies of Jordan, Saudi Arabia and Pakistan. Note the air portable undercarriage skids and the specially filtered engine intakes.

Top left: Aérospatiale has developed the SA 365M Dauphin into a multi-role helicopter using the very best of equipment available from the French helicopter industry, including HOT missiles and the SFIM sight, the Giat 20mm cannon pod and Crouzet or Thomson-CSF gun sights. The new helicopter is called the Panther. (Brian Walters/United Writers' Group)

Bottom left: The SA 365M Panther can be armed with the Giat 20mm gun pod for close support and escort duties. It is possible that the helicopter will be acquired by the French ALAT until the Eurocopter HAC is delivered. (Brian Walters/United Writers' Group)

Top right: During the Falklands conflict, British Army Gazelle helicopters were armed with SNEB rocket pods as much to give confidence to the aircrew as to combat the enemy. The conflict proved the need for armed observation/reconnaissance helicopters. (Author's collection)

Centre Right: Operated by the Argentine forces in the Falklands, this Agusta A109A was captured by 3 Commando Brigade Air Squadron, Royal Marines, and pressed into British service. It has since been modified for British Army service. (Author's collection)

Bottom right: The first of the new generation of light attack helicopters to fly, the Agusta A129 Mangusta, seen here during development flying in Italy. The first aircraft join the Italian Army in 1987 and a developed version, the Tonal, is being studied by the UK, Italy, Spain and The Netherlands.

Top left: Agusta's Mangusta will carry TOW, HOT or Hellfire anti-tank missiles, depending on the customer's preference and existing inventories. Note the mast-mounted sight and twin Rolls-Royce 1004 engines. The helicopter is armed with eight TOW and a rocket launcher.

Centre left: A field briefing site for a PAH-1 *schwarm*-level anti-tank operation. Note the dispersed helicopters and fact that on this exercise nuclear-biological-chemical warfare protective clothing is not being worn. (Author's collection)

Bottom left: From 1986, BO 105P will be equipped with a new six-launcher system for the HOT, which, being triangular in shape, allows the helicopter better performance in hover especially on hot days. The missiles in these launchers are the new HOT-2 with the same basic dimensions as HOT but having a better warhead and greater range. (Author's collection)

Top right: Federal Germany's anti-tank defence is supplemented by three regiments of MBB PAH-1 (BO 105P) light attack helicopters which each carry six Euromissile HOT wire-guided anti-tank missiles. (Author's collection)

Opposite, bottom left: Spain's FAMET is an enthusiastic user of the BO 105P attack helicopter, also using the HOT missile system. The helicopters were built under licence by CASA in Madrid and are operated by the anti-tank helicopter battalion of the Spanish Army near Cuidad Real. (Author's collection)

Opposite, bottom right: British Army Lynx aircrew specialize in low flying and nap-of-the-earth exercises from their bases in Germany. British Army of the Rhine operates three regiments of mixed Lynx and Gazelle units to defend the 1 (British) Corps area against tank invasion. This Lynx is moving under the wires of a high-tension line – to fly over them would lead to identification and the possibility of being shot down. (Author's collection)

Bell's AH-1W SuperCobra is the first attack helicopter to be able to fire the TOW or Hellfire missiles, and a production helicopter is seen here with Hellfire rounds on the stub-wing pylons. Hellfire is a laser-guided missile which is also fitted to the Apache.

Top left: Moving low across a corn field in central Germany, this Lynx from 4 Regiment, Army Air Corps, is approaching a HELARM firing position. Squadron or even Regimental anti-tank actions have been practised on large exercises such as 'Lionheart'. (Author's collection)

Centre left: In 1986, British Army of the Rhine helicopters commenced an experiment to test a new colour scheme of grey and green in the continued effort to make the helicopters merge into the background while hovering and during low-level cross-country flight. Gazelles have also been painted in the same colours. (Author's collection)

Bottom left: Giving the barest armed helicopter ability, the FFV rocket-armed Agusta-Bell 206 of the Swedish Army Aviation will soon be replaced by the BO 105CS armed with Saab-Emerson HeliTOW. The 206 will then be used for armed reconnaissance on the flanks of the battlefield.

Opposite, top: The standard US Army air cavalry attack team is the scouting Kiowa (right), supported by the armed Bell AH-1Q Cobra attack helicopter (from an Army National Guard Unit) shown here armed with 70mm rocket pods and equipped with an anti-IR missile engine exhaust cowling. (US DoD)

Opposite, Centre: TOW firing during Exercise 'Bright Star '84' in Egypt when the 82nd Airborne Division supported Egyptian and American forces in a major rapid deployment force exercise. Note the dust displaced by the hovering AH-1S Cobra helicopters. (US DoD)

Opposite, bottom left: In a modern battle, all arms work together. This is an exercise for a US Army Joint Air Attack Team which consists of the Kiowa/Cobra fire team to kill the tanks, with the A-10A Thunderbolt II ground attack aircraft to distract the enemy self-propelled anti-aircraft defences. These aircraft are seen during an exercise in Hawaii in 1985. (US DoD)

Opposite, bottom right: A Hawaiian National Guard ground-crewman loads 70mm Hydra rocket rounds into the rocket launcher of a AH-1S Cobra; Rockets tend to be used against soft targets and for fire support sorties to suppress enemy activity around a landing zone. (US DoD)

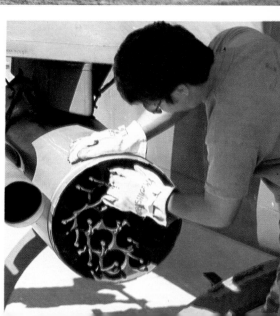

Top left: Hawaiian National Guard Cobra prepare for a day's action. The Bell AH-1S Cobra, as it stands, is not capable of night fighting but is being modified to take the C-NITE infra-red sighting system. This helicopter is fitted for but not with radar warning receivers. (US DoD)

Bottom left: A typical attack helicopter weapon load. This AH-1S Cobra is carrying four Hughes Aircraft TOW missiles (this helicopter is unarmed for an air show) and 19 fin-folding aerial rockets per side on the stub wing mountings. Both weapon systems can be easily reloaded in the field. (Author's collection)

Top right: US Army Europe Cobra are armed with the 20mm Gatling chin-mounted machine-gun and the nose-mounted M65 sight for TOW anti-tank missiles. The co-pilot/gunner's sight assembly can be seen through the front cockpit canopy. (Author's collection)

Right: As an interim fit before acquiring the new AH-1S Cobra, the US Army modified the AH-1G (of Vietnam fame) to AH-1Q standard to carry TOW but not having the modern systems and fittings, including the angular cockpit canopy. These Hawaiian Army National Guard helicopters are some of the last AH-1Q helicopters in service. (US DoD)

Far right: Three AH-1S Cobra wait to be called into action during an anti-tank exercise in southern Germany. European-based Cobra have the latest weapons and electronic warfare fits, including IR missile jammers and radar warning receivers. (Author's collection)

Left: To supplement and improve upon the Cobra in the attack role, the US Army began introducing the McDonnell Douglas AH-64A Apache into service in April 1986. The advanced attack helicopter is capable of night/day and adverse weather operations, carrying the latest Hellfire laser-guided anti-armour missiles and the 30mm Hughes chain gun. (MCDHC)

Top right: To assemble the Apache, McDonnell Douglas built a completely new facility at Mesa, Arizona. There are more than twenty suppliers to the AAH programme, including Martin-Marietta who make the target acquisition and designation system/pilot's night vision system, and Teledyne which constructs the fuselage. (MCDHC)

Bottom right: As part of its search to find a new light attack helicopter, the US Army has contracted the top US manufacturers to examine future concepts. McDonnell Douglas is using an YAH-64 prototype Apache to examine various aspects of single-pilot operation for the so-called LHX-SCAT.

Left: With its eye firmly set on the export market, Sikorsky Aircraft has developed the Eagle from its executive helicopter, the S-76. The Eagle is designed as a multi-role helicopter and is seen here as a light transport, but takes less than 30 minutes to convert to an armed helicopter with guns, rockets or missiles. (Sikorsky via Frank Colucci)

Below: The H-76 Eagle seen during early flight trials in Connecticut; standard weaponry includes the Hughes Aircraft TOW anti-tank missiles. The helicopter may form the basis of a US-Brazilian agreement to set up a fully fledged helicopter manufacturing industry in Brazil, and the helicopter is seen as having export potential around the world.

European Attack Helicopters

All four major helicopter manufacturers in Europe – Aérospatiale (France), Agusta (Italy), MBB (Federal Germany) and Westland (United Kingdom) – have been involved in the development and production of attack helicopters. By far the largest manufacturer in terms of helicopters made and sales is Aérospatiale, the company offering a range of light to medium attack helicopters with a dedicated tandem-seat attack helicopter in development with Federal Germany.

The current Aérospatiale product line consists of the AS 350L1 Ecureuil and the AS 355M2 Ecureuil 2, both fitted with cannon, machine-guns or rockets for light attack duties. The principle cannon system is the Giat M621 20mm system, often carried with the Thomson-Brandt Armement's 68mm rocket system, which can be fitted with anti-tank kinetic darts as well as more conventional warheads. Moving up the scale, the SA 342 Gazelle is still in production, although in 1986 lines were only open in Yugoslavia (SOKO) and Egypt (Anglo-Arab Helicopters). Gazelle is the current armed reconnaissance and anti-tank helicopter of a number of forces, having seen action with the French ALAT (in Chad), the Syrians (during the Lebanon invasion), Iraq (against Iranian armoured vehicles) and Morocco (against the Polisario). For armed reconnaissance, the Gazelle can be armed with the Giat cannon, Thomson-Brandt or several other types of rockets, but several nations have fitted the Euromissile HOT and, in the case of Yugoslavia, Soviet-made anti-tank missiles.

In 1986, Aérospatiale revealed the SA 365M Panther derivative of the existing Dauphin 2 range of helicopters. The French have high hopes for the Panther, which is powered by the new Turboméca TM333-1M turboshaft engine and is capable of maximum cruising speed of about 150 knots (278km/h). Aérospatiale is marketing the helicopter as a multi-mission helicopter with three distinct attack helicopter roles: fire support, anti-tank and anti-helicopter. For the fire support role, two 20mm pod-mounted cannon and two 68mm rocket launchers with a total of 44 rounds can be carried. These are exchanged for the HOT and HOT-2 anti-tank missiles for day or night anti-tank operations, while if there is a helicopter threat, the helicopter can be fitted with eight new Matra Mistral air-to-air missiles and two 20mm pod-mounted cannon. The Company states that the Panther can be converted from a commando assault role to that of an attack helicopter in 45 minutes.

Until the mid 1970s, Italy's state-owned helicopter manufacturer, Agusta, had not been directly involved in attack helicopters, but following a request from the Italian ALE (army light aviation), the Company began development of the A129A Mangusta. To allow anti-tank missile and tactical experience to be built up, the A109 executive helicopter was re-configured as an interim anti-tank helicopter for the Italian ALE. In addition, the A109 sold overseas, including a number for the Argentine Army which used the rocket and machine-gun armed helicopter against British forces in the Falklands; two of the helicopters were captured and pressed into British Army service supporting, with two specially purchased, the Special Air Service Regiment, according to press reports.

Agusta offers the A109 with various calibre rockets, light 7.62mm podded machine-guns, 12.7mm guns, air-to-air missiles or both Euromissile HOT and Hughes Aircraft TOW anti-tank missiles. For a light attack mission, the helicopter can carry two 12.7mm podded guns and fourteen 68mm rockets in pods, but for an anti-tank sortie, the helicopter is re-configured with the Hughes M65 chin-mounted sight and TOW missiles. It is now possible to fit night vision equipment to the helicopter, using various manufacturers' thermal-imaging modules. A typical anti-tank sortie for the A109 would be to fly 50nm (93km), spend 90 minutes on station (including 45 minutes in the hover to stalk and engage targets) before returning to base; according to Hughes Aircraft the TOW system is 98 per cent accurate when fired by a trained operator from the Agusta A109.

The attack helicopter experience being developed with the A109 has been transferred to the A129 programme, with the helicopter due to enter service in mid 1987. The A129 is the first of the new generation European dedicated light attack helicopter projects to fly, is powered by two Rolls-Royce Gem engines and fitted with the Harris Corporation multiplex system to integrate the weapons, sensors and avionic features to reduce pilot workload. It first flew in 1983 and has been developed for service entry with the ALE, and was chosen in 1986 for further development by the UK, Dutch, Spanish and Italian governments for a future light attack helicopter.

In action, the A129 can deliver a substantial firepower of machine-gun, cannon, rocket or missile type. Typical weapon loads include eight TOW or eight TOW and 14 68/70mm rockets, a total of 52 rockets or 38 rockets and two podded 12.7mm guns. Development of the helicopter to fire the laser-designated Rockwell Hellfire, the Matra Mistral and General Dynamics Stinger is underway; if the British Army selects the developed A129 (called Tonal by the Italians and A129 Mk 2 by the British), it may be fitted with the Shorts Starstreak air-to-air missile.

When the Federal German Bundeswehr called for an anti-tank helicopter to support the armoured divisions defending the Inner German Border against invasion from the east, MBB (Messerschmitt-Bölkow-Blohm) responded with a developed version of the BO 105 rigid-rotor helicopter. In 1974, the BO 105M was selected for the liaison and scout role and a year later, the BO 105P (known as the PAH-1 or Panzerabwehr Hubschrauber 1) was selected as the attack helicopter, armed with HOT missiles for the anti-tank role. The PAH-1 has an endurance of more than two hours and can carry six HOT missiles; it is operated in *schwarme* of seven helicopters, operating in concert with tanks and other direct fire elements of the ground army.

By September 1984, all 312 BO 105 (212 of them PAH-1 versions) had been delivered to the Heeresflieger for service with the Northern Armoured Division and the three army corps in the NATO Central Region. The Germans also support the Belgian and Dutch forces, both countries still awaiting the introduction of their first attack helicopters.

Although German BO 105 have not been in action, those supplied elsewhere are thought to have seen conflict. For example, a number have entered service with the Iraqi Army for use against Iranian tanks and other targets, those locally assembled by PADC in The Philippines have been used for light attack duties against the Communist rebels, and it is possible that some of the NBO 105 built by PT IPTN, the Indonesian aircraft industry, have been operated against rebels and guerrilla forces in Timor. Other users include the Spanish FAMET and the Swedish Army which both have missile-armed versions (the former with the HOT and the latter with HeliTOW).

In conjunction with Kawasaki Heavy Industries in Japan, MBB has developed the basic 105 airframe into the larger and more powerful BK 117 design which was shown at the 1985 Paris Air Show as an attack helicopter. Although no orders have been taken for the BK 117A-3M version, armed with HOT or TOW missiles and carrying the 12.7mm Lucas Aerospace gun mounting, the helicopter does show some interesting developments, including radar warning receivers, mission management computers, the mast-mounted sight and the ability to role change rapidly, rather in the same way as the Panther and Sikorsky Eagle. The BK 117 is another example of the cost-effective combat support helicopter which can take on the role of an attack helicopter as part of a multi-role package; this has appeal to nations lacking sufficient funds to buy a dedicated attack helicopter.

In the United Kingdom, the British Army of the Rhine requested an updated attack helicopter to replace the Scout/SS11 interim fit which had been deployed to various units in the late 1960s and early 1970s. Funding restrictions prevented the development of a dedicated attack helicopter and it was decided to adopt the Hughes Aircraft TOW anti-tank missile and fit it to the Westland Lynx AH 1 utility helicopter. The French government pulled out of a development programme, originally set up under the 1967 Anglo-French Helicopter Agreement, to develop a tandem-seat dedicated attack helicopter using the Lynx dynamics and the Rolls-Royce Gem powerplant.

More than 100 Lynx AH 1 and some 24 Lynx AH 7 helicopters are currently in service, serving in the attack helicopter role in Germany and to a certain extent in the United Kingdom. Although Lynx operate in Northern Ireland, they are only used for utility support purposes and do not carry armament. To fit the two four-round TOW launchers, a new mounting was attached to the helicopter's fuselage, and British Aerospace developed the Hughes Aircraft M65 sight for placing in the helicopter's roof. In 1986, BAe and Rank Pullin Controls were given a contract to update about 100 Lynx with thermal-imaging modules to make them fully night firing capable. Until the TI modules were fitted the helicopters were limited to daylight only attack tasks although naturally they were able to fly from place to place at night, using instrument flight rules (higher altitude) or night vision goggle equipment.

In August 1986, the development Lynx fitted with the new BERP rotor blades broke the world absolute speed record, reaching 216 knots (400km/h). In 1982, Westland announced the Lynx-3 attack helicopter (with some limited multi-role ability) which it hoped the British Army would acquire to replace the existing Lynx force, becoming the Light Attack Helicopter. However, the UK's Army Air Corps required a dedicated, possibly tandem-seated attack helicopter (such as the AH-64 Apache or A129 Mangusta) and so Westland has been marketing the helicopter to Middle and Far Eastern nations.

Lynx-3 can be armed with the HOT, TOW or Hellfire anti-tank missiles and the Stinger, Mistral or Starstreak air-to-air missiles. It first flew in June 1984, powered by two Rolls-Royce Gem 60 turboshafts (similar to those used by the A129 and Westland 30). It is heavier, faster and better protected than the Lynx

AH 1/7 series, but the British Army did not think that it was enough of an improvement over the latter to warrant development for them.

FRENCH-DESIGNED ATTACK HELICOPTERS

Manufacturer	**Aérospatiale**
Model	**AS 350L Ecureuil**
Service entry	1985
Engines	1 × Arriel
Crew	1/2
Gross weight	1950kg (4299lb)
Max speed	147 knots (272km/h)
Range	378nm (700km)
Weapons	1 × Giat 20mm or 70mm rocket launchers

Manufacturer	**Aérospatiale**
Model	**SA 319B Alouette III**
Service entry	1969
Engines	1 × Astazou XIVB
Crew	2
Gross weight	2250kg (4960lb)
Max speed	118 knots (220km/h)
Range	340nm (630km)
Weapons	4 × AS 11 or 2 × AS 12 missiles; 2 × 7.62mm or 12.7mm or 20mm guns; 70mm rocket launchers

Manufacturer	**Aérospatiale**
Model	**SA 342L Gazelle**
Service entry	1976
Engines	1 × Astazou XIVH
Crew	2
Gross weight	1900kg (4190lb)
Max speed	167 knots (310km/h)
Range	407nm (755km)
Weapons	4 or 6 × HOT anti-tank missiles; 1 × Giat 20mm; 70mm rocket launchers

Manufacturer	**Aérospatiale**
Model	**SA 365M Panther**
Service entry	(awaiting orders)
Engines	2 × Arriel 520M
Crew	2
Gross weight	3900kg (8600lb)
Max speed	165 knots (306km/h)
Range	410nm (758km)
Weapons	8 × HOT/TOW anti-tank missiles; 70mm rocket launchers; 7.62mm, 12.7mm or 20mm gun pods; flares and chaff

102. Although used by a number of nations for liaison, VIP transport and observation tasks, several users of the SA 342 Gazelle have mounted anti-tank missiles on the helicopter. This is believed to be a Moroccan Gazelle, armed with Euromissile HOT and photographed prior to delivery.

GERMAN-DESIGNED ATTACK HELICOPTERS

Manufacturer	**Messerschmitt-Bölkow-Blohm**
Model	**BO 105P (PAH-1)**
Service entry	1980
Engines	2 × Allison 250-C20B
Crew	2
Gross weight	2400kg (5291lb)
Max speed	145 knots (269km/h)
Range	407nm (754km)
Weapons	6 × HOT or 8 × TOW anti-tank missiles; 20mm Rh 202 cannon; 70mm rocket launchers

ITALIAN-DESIGNED ATTACK HELICOPTERS

Manufacturer	**Agusta**
Model	**A129 Mangusta**
Service entry	1987
Engines	2 × Rolls-Royce Gem 2-2
Crew	2
Gross weight	3800kg (8377lb)
Max speed	150 knots (278km/h)
Range	400nm (741km)
Weapons	6/8 × HOT/TOW/Hellfire anti-tank missiles; 12.7mm

or 20mm gun mountings; 70mm rocket launchers

BRITISH-DESIGNED ATTACK HELICOPTERS

Manufacturer	**Westland**
Model	**Lynx AH 1**
Service entry	1977
Engines	2 × Rolls-Royce Gem
Gross weight	4535kg (10000lb)
Max speed	160 knots (296km/h)
Range	340nm (630km)
Weapons	8 × TOW anti-tank missiles; SNORA 70mm rocket launchers

Manufacturer	**Westland**
Model	**Lynx-3**
Service entry	(awaiting orders)
Engines	2 × Rolls-Royce Gem 60-3
Gross weight	5897kg (13000lb)
Max speed	161 knots (298km/h)
Range	373nm (691km)
Weapons	8 × TOW-2/Hellfire anti-tank missiles with Stinger air-to-air missiles; 70mm rocket launchers; 20mm Oerlikon cannon; other ordnance

103. The thermal-imaging system for the Lynx is being developed to operate in the far infra-red waveband, enabling the attack helicopter to engage armoured targets in low-light, night or conditions when the target is visually obscured by mist, dust or smoke on the battlefield during the day. (BAe)

104. Bridging the gap between scout and light attack helicopter, the AS 355M2 Ecureuil 2 is being marketed by Aérospatiale, especially to African nations, several of which have purchased a cannon-armed version for light attack and border security duties. This picture actually shows the helicopter in a commando role. (Aérospatiale)

105. The Gazelle can be armed with up to six HOT missiles which have a range of 3.75km (2.3 miles), and like the TOW system, HOT is wire-guided and optically tracked through a roof-mounted sight, manufactured in France by SFIM. In this picture it can be seen mounted above the gunner's position on the port side of the helicopter.

▲104   ▼105

106. Pictured on the Suippes ranges in eastern France, this SA 342K Gazelle of the French ALAT is conducting firing trials with the Euromissile HOT. The French Army's helicopters carry four HOT per sortie and are used directly to support the army tank units or for the Force d'Action Rapide (rapid deployment force) which could be sent anywhere in the world. (Euromissile)

107. In Yugoslavia, the State Aircraft Factory, SOKO, manufactures the Gazelle under licence. There are at least 130 Gazelle in service in the country and many are armed with the AT-3 Swatter optically-guided anti-tank missile as illustrated here. Note the Mi-8 Hip transport helicopters in the background. (SOKO)

108. As a follow-on to the Gazelle, Aérospatiale experimented with the Dauphin helicopter, especially in developing the ability to operate and fight at night – the so-called 24-hour battle. This SA 361 Dauphin is armed with eight containerized HOT missiles with a day-only SFIM sight in the cabin roof and a SFIM Venus forward-looking infra-red gimbal-mounted sensor on the chin.

109. In 1986, Aérospatiale announced the re-naming and improvement of the Dauphin for the multi-role, but predominantly for attack helicopter tasks. Called the Panther, the new helicopter is powered by the TM 333 engine and can be armed with a variety of weapons including a podded Giat 20mm cannon as illustrated here.

▲108 ▼109

110. For the day/night attack role, the Panther can be armed with eight HOT missiles using the SFIM Vivianne direct view and thermal-imaging, roof-mounted sight. Aérospatiale hope to interest the French ALAT in purchasing the helicopter as an interim before the next generation of dedicated attack helicopters.

111. The Panther's range of weaponry displayed at the Marseilles factory. From left to right: Giat 20mm cannon, Thomson Brandt 70mm rockets, FN Zeebrugges 70mm rockets, HOT and TOW anti-tank missiles. All these weapons have an attack role and can be used against light to heavy tanks, armoured vehicles, trucks or bunker positions.

110▲ 111▼

▲112

112. Aérospatiale's development of the Panther has included the ability to carry airborne survivability equipment such as radar warning receivers, chaff/flare launchers and IR jammers to defeat incoming heat-seeking missiles. The airframe is agile and manoeuvrable, but also has the ability to carry up to ten troops.

113. Operated in a light attack role during the
▼113

Falklands conflict, the Agusta A109A Hirundo is armed with a 7.62mm podded machine-gun and seven 68mm rockets on each side of the fuselage. This example was captured by the Royal Marines, impressed into service and later displayed at Middle Wallop Air Day 1982. It has since been refurbished and taken on strength by HQ 7 Regiment, Army Air Corps, for special detached duties. (Author's collection)

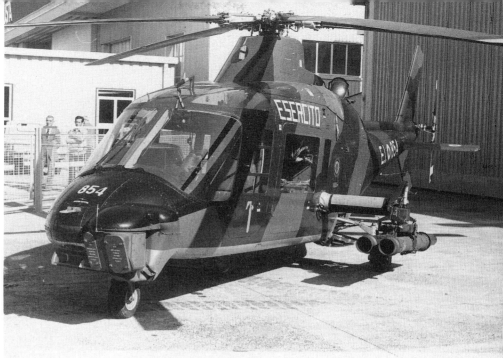

114. As an interim development, Agusta and the Italian ALE have armed the A109 Mk II with the TOW missile system, using the chin-mounted M65 sight. This helicopter has been providing useful data for the A129 attack helicopter programme. (Author's collection)

115. Flying in the Alps near Milan, this A109 Mk II is one of several now in service with the Italian forces. The helicopter is fast and responsive, giving a good indication of the A129's performance as the ALE develops its tactics for fighting against an armoured invasion from north, east or south. (Agusta)

114▲

115▼

▲116

116. Taken aloft for the first time in September 1983, the A129 Mangusta is an Italian design with British engines and American integrated electronics. It is a light attack helicopter, but the first built in Europe with tandem seating and a dedicated battlefield role. (Agusta)

117. The thin forward profile of the A129 is very important in the battlefield environment and adds to the survivability of the helicopter. In addition, Agusta has built-in tolerances for the vital systems against 12.7mm rounds and the helicopter should be agile enough to avoid combat if necessary. (Author's collection)

118. The Mangusta is powered by two Rolls-Royce Gem 2 Mk 1004 engines in its Mk 1 version for the Italian Army. The British engine manufacturer heavily supported the flight test programme at Cossina

Costa near Milan. In this photograph notice also the round escape hatches for the test pilots and the nose-mounted Hughes Aircraft M65 TOW sight. (Rolls-Royce)

119. To increase survivability, the A129 is powered by two engines, one on each side of the fuselage, so that damage to one powerplant will not necessarily cause the other to lose power. Note also the stub wings with the two stores attachments on each side. (Agusta)

120. For a longer endurance attack task, the A129 will carry eight TOW rounds on the outboard pylons and then has a loiter time of several hours. Note the addition of the night vision sensor to the nose of this development model and the clear view for the pilot sitting in the rear seat.

▼117

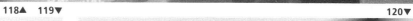

118▲ 119▼ 120▼

▲121

▲122   ▼123

121. Flying through typical northern Italian woodland, the Agusta A129 development helicopter is tested for its ability to work in confined areas, among the trees, and to make use of natural features for cover. In action, it would be expected to wait in ambush for tanks coming into the open.

122. If the helicopter is hit and has to make a forced landing, the undercarriage arrangement and the use of Martin-Baker crashworthy seats should ensure that the helicopter and its crew survive to fight another day.

123. The Gem engine is relatively small, but develops sufficient power to give the A129 a cruising speed of about 143 knots (265km/h); but for the attack helicopter the need is usually to fly slowly, nap-of-the-earth with sufficient power to dash to or from a target as required. The Mk 2 version of the helicopter, which might be developed by the British, Dutch, Spanish and Italian armies, could have a single large engine instead of two smaller types. (Rolls-Royce)

124. The Mangusta's range of weaponry: on the helicopter are two four-missile TOW launchers and two 7–round 70mm rocket launchers. Additional armament includes two 19-round 70mm rocket launchers and two podded 7.62mm or 12.7mm machine-guns. In the foreground is the laser-designated Hellfire missile system; it is thought that six of them could be carried on a developed version. (Agusta)

▲125

▲126　▼127

125. In the light attack and close support roles, the A129 Mangusta could be equipped with the 19-round rocket launcher to engage softer targets than tanks. This weapon would be useful if the helicopter were to be used in the armed reconnaissance role.

126. All attack helicopters have to be agile and the A129 is no exception; it is also considered to be quiet and easily concealed. Its future development could be vital to the NATO anti-tank defence strategy of the next twenty years. (Rolls-Royce)

127. In Italian service, it is hoped that the A129 will be developed to carry a mast-mounted sight with laser designation and rangefinding equipment which will enable the Hellfire missile to be carried. IR jammers and radar warning antennae are also fitted to this model. (Beaver/Downey collection)

128. The secret of successful attack helicopter operations lies in the integration of the airborne with the ground-based formations. The Federal German Bundeswehr has become extremely good at co-operation between direct-fire arms, such as the attack helicopter (PAH-1) and the ground-based Marder anti-tank/armed reconnaissance units. (MBB).

129. In 1975, the Bundeswehr selected the BO 105 airframe to be developed into the PAH-1 (first generation anti-tank helicopter) for service with the three German Corps on the NATO Central Front and with the Northern Division. Some 212 PAH-1 were delivered between 1980–4. Each PAH-1 is armed with six Euromissile HOT anti-tank missiles.

128▲ 129▼

▲130

▲131 ▼132

130. HOT was developed by the Franco-German Euromissile Company which is jointly owned by Aérospatiale and MBB. The missile has sold well and is particularly appealing to attack helicopter users because it is easy to reload and handle in the field. This is the standard pre-1987 launcher configuration; the new system has a triangular shape to assist aerodynamics.

131. Weekly training is necessary, but live missile rounds are expensive. The Heeresflieger (army aviation) has acquired a number of specialist training devices, including the TALISSI system with its simulated missile firing using a laser system.

132. In the PAH-1, the captain/gunner sits with the sight and missile launcher equipment on the helicopter's port side; the HOT missile has proved very reliable in service and for the trained operator it has an accuracy of about 98 per cent. Like TOW, HOT is wire-guided.

133. PAH-1 helicopters operate in *schwarme* of seven helicopters, defending portions of the Inner German Border in co-operation with ground forces. The PAH-1 units operate almost every day, even in winter, in order to keep training standards high. The SFIM APX M397 sight can be seen on the cabin roof. (MBB)

134. The green-and-black camouflage pattern of the PAH-1 is very effective in the wooded areas of northern and southern Germany, but it is likely that anti-tank operations would be carried out in built-up areas as well. The PAH-1 has a two-man team of captain (gunner/commander) and pilot.

133▲   134▼

135. In the defence of German soil, the PAH-1 units have learned the best and most tactically advantageous ambush positions from which to engage enemy tank formations. The standard *modus operandi* is for the helicopters to engage command tanks in the rear of an assault and for ground forces to attack the anti-aircraft and lead tanks.

136. The PAH-1's rotor system has been modified to give better anti-vibration performance, but it is checked by the pilot before each flight. On the outbreak of war, the helicopters would immediately depart from their peacetime bases (like Celle here) to field locations.

137. Because a great deal of time is spent hovering in trees and along other natural features, the PAH-1 is given the twin-engined safety of two Allison 250 engines. The helicopter is considered an interim development before the next generation (PAH-2) is brought into service in the mid 1990s. (Author's collection)

138. The Spanish FAMET is the largest foreign customer for the military BO 105 and most of the helicopters were built by CASA in Madrid. Current Spanish inventory is 28 missile-armed and 18 20mm cannon-armed attack helicopters; others from the Spanish line have been delivered to Iraq and possibly some South American customers. (CASA)

137▲   138▼

▲139

▲140 ▼141

139, 140. Although both Federal Germany and Spain have been operating the HOT-armed BO 105 for some years, the Swedish Army decided that the TOW missile represented the optimum solution to its attack helicopter requirement. These two pictures show the initial configuration of the TOW, using standard launchers and the Saab HeliTOW sight. Note the use of the green/brown/black splinter camouflage pattern also seen on Royal Swedish Air Force fixed-wing aircraft.

141. The BO 105C (HkP-9A to the Swedes) has now entered service with the Saab-Emerson HeliTOW system which includes special TOW launchers and the Saab sighting system. There is a strong possibility that the sight will be augmented for night operations using the Ericsson thermal-imaging module in 1987. This picture was taken in late 1985 during missile firing tests. (Emerson Electric)

142. Developed from the executive and medical transport BK 117, the A-3M version was shown for the first time at the 1985 Paris Air Show and features eight HOT missiles and the Lucas Aerospace 12.7mm gun turret in this mock-up view. Note the mast-mounted sight and roof-mounted system, as well as radar warning receivers. (MBB)

142▶

▲143 ▼144

143. Operating with the Queen's Royal Irish Hussars (Chieftain tanks), this UK Army Air Corps Lynx AH 1 helicopter demonstrates how important it is for full co-operation between tank (ground) and helicopter (air) assets to defeat enemy tank and armoured assaults. The Lynx is mainly deployed to three regiments supporting 1 (BR) Corps in Germany.

144. Westland Lynx AH 1 is armed with the Hughes Aircraft TOW anti-tank missile system, illustrated here. The missile fins deploy on launching, when the missile is tracked through the roof-mounted sight (not visible) and guided by two thin wires. Reloads can be carried inside the helicopter's cabin. (R. D. M. Sharpe)

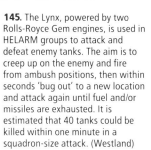

145. The Lynx, powered by two Rolls-Royce Gem engines, is used in HELARM groups to attack and defeat enemy tanks. The aim is to creep up on the enemy and fire from ambush positions, then within seconds 'bug out' to a new location and attack again until fuel and/or missiles are exhausted. It is estimated that 40 tanks could be killed within one minute in a squadron-size attack. (Westland)

146. In Germany, the main flying technique is nap-of-the-earth, using the ground contours and other natural features (as well as buildings) to mask the helicopter from an enemy formation until the helicopter is ready to fire. Low flying is, therefore, practised regularly even in peacetime. (Rolls-Royce)

▲147   ▼148

147. HOT is also capable of being fired by the Lynx AH 1, but in the ordinary course of events the helicopter's fire control and sighting systems would have to be totally reconfigured to allow for the system. It is not possible to interchange HOT and TOW missiles. (Westland)

148,149. A sequenced pair of photographs showing a TOW engagement during trials with the system in the early 1980s. There is no real sensation when the missile is fired, but the pilot must keep the helicopter within the missile's launch constraints during its 17-second time of flight to the target. (Westland)

150. During the years that Lynx/TOW has been in service, there have been a series of modifications to the missile system, including the improvement of the missile (I-TOW) and the proposed top-attack fuzing system, developed by Thorn EMI Electronics to give the missile the ability to engage a target and cause the blast to act downwards through vulnerable upper armour. (Westland)

▲151 ▼152

151. Besides the Army Air Corps, Britain's Royal Marines also operate a small number of Lynx AH 1 to provide attack helicopter support to the units which might be called upon to defend Northern Norway against invasion from the east. For the snow role, the Lynx can be equipped with bearpad snow skids. (Westland)

152, 153. Despite the small number of helicopters available, the Royal Marines have become very skilled in the use of the Lynx in all weather conditions. There are dangers to any helicopter from ice forming on the airframe and rotor surfaces, as well as from re-circulation through the engine intakes. RM aircrew wear special protective clothing and survival gear. (RN/HMS *Heron* by B. M. Cartwright)

154. As part of the Lynx AH 1 mid-life improvement package, British Aerospace and Rank Pullin Controls have been awarded a contract to fit a thermal-imaging system in the HAC/BAe TOW roof-sight to give night firing ability to the helicopter. Until 1987 (when the first system comes into service), the Army Air Corps has been the only direct fire arm of the British Army without the capability to fight at night. (BAe)

155. The Lynx-3 design was refined in 1982–84 with the addition of Hellfire missiles and the General Dynamics Stinger system for self-defence against air targets, including enemy helicopters and close air support. (Westland)

156. The Lynx-3 development helicopter does not have the mast-mounted sight, but uses either the BAe or Saab roof sight. It is armed in this picture with eight Rockwell hellfire missiles and two twin Stinger launchers on a special fuselage launcher. It first flew in June 1984.

▲155   ▼156

Soviet
Attack Helicopters

To understand the current Soviet trend in large, high-speed attack helicopters, one has to understand the battlefield tactics and doctrine which have prevailed in the Soviet Red Army since the enormous battles of the 'Great Patriotic War' of 1942–5. The open plains of the Russian steppe, between Europe and the Ural Mountains, stretch for about 1,000 miles (1,610km) and, devoid of tree cover, it is no place for hovering attack helicopters but rather is suited to close air support. Furthermore, it is over this terrain that the Soviets think they would have to fight to defend the country's industrial heartland – they are still convinced that the western Europeans are bent on invasion.

The development of the attack helicopter started with the Mi-8 Hip as an armed assault helicopter capable of attacking enemy positions and following up the fusillade of cannon and rocket fire with assault troops specially trained in this airmobile role. As demonstrated to the Israeli forces when the Egyptians crossed the Suez Canal in the early hours of the Yom Kippur war (1973), it is a fearsome sight to see a large number of heavy armed attack helicopters looming out of the smoke of the initial artillery barrage, providing their own suppressive power with up to 192 57mm rockets and yet carrying some 20 fully armed troops into battle. The Hip-E is acknowledged by the US armed forces as being the first heavily armed attack helicopter in the world; it is still in production and almost 2,000 are now deployed to Soviet and Warsaw Pact forces.

From the Mi-8 series, which also includes a range of communications, electronic warfare and other interesting sub-variants, has come perhaps the world's most famous attack helicopter, the Hind. This helicopter, more correctly known as the Mi-24, held the world absolute helicopter speed record for eight years from September 1978 (it was beaten by a Westland Lynx in August 1986), but it stems from the border war between the Soviet Union and the People's Republic of China in the late 1960s. Apparently it became clear to the Russian commanders that they needed a weapon like the Sturmovik of the 'Great Patriotic War', with its ability to carry a large amount of weaponry, have good speed and endurance and be armoured against counter-attack. In other words, the Russian commanders were looking for a flying tank.

The flying tank allowed battlefield commanders to bring direct fire on strategic points in minutes rather than hours. The Russians were quick to notice the flexibility and agility of the attack helicopter for the modern battlefield. The Hind probably took in the lessons of the Cobra (tandem seating) and the S-67 Blackhawk project (a US Army helicopter which did not enter service), but it stems more from the development of helicopters by the Mil design bureau and the needs of the Soviet forces.

The first Hind was the B variant (NATO observers were a little confused about the helicopter at the time), but it was the A variant (the improved second production model) that was seen for the first time over East Germany in 1974. These two variants, together with the C training version, were the initial developments, but were delivered to the Soviet, East German, Algerian and Libyan forces.

In 1971, the Soviet defence ministry ordered a re-design of the Hind to give it a more survivable appearance, better sighting systems and, above all, better weapons. The Hind-D appeared in 1975 and some 1,000 have been built since, delivered to Warsaw Pact and Soviet client states, including those in combat in Afghanistan, Nicaragua, Angola and Iraq.

The Hind-D is a two/three-seat helicopter, with an NCO gunner in the front cockpit, a pilot behind and in the cabin there is a flight engineer in some variants. There is also room for eight fully armed combat troops for commando-style operations; some late Model D and the succeeding E do not as a rule carry troops. The Hind-D is armed with a 12.7mm chin-mounted, four-barrelled rotary cannon on a gimbal mounting, plus provision for 64 57mm rockets on the stud wing launchers, with the addition of the radar-guided AT-2 Swatter and AT-3 Sagger anti-tank missiles on wing-tip pylons. These additions are rarely seen in photographs published in the West.

In 1980 the Soviet forces introduced the Hind-E, with the twin GSh-23L 23mm cannon on the starboard forward fuselage and uprated with the anti-tank missiles to the AT-6 Spiral, a second-generation tube-launched system which many observers believe could be used for anti-helicopter operations. It is aimed via a laser designator on the pylon end. The exact designation of Soviet

157. The Hip-C does not have the fire control and sighting system necessary for the radar, radio or wire-guided anti-tank missiles of the Hip-H, but it does carry a very heavy punch of some 128 57mm rockets (from four launcher sets) and a fixed 12.7mm gun firing forward. As usual with Soviet types, good clear photographs are difficult to find in the West.

helicopters is very difficult to establish and all that is really known is that the Soviets call the Hind the Mi-24, but the actual model numbers are secret except that the world record holder was called A-10. It is, therefore, difficult to know whether there is a Hind-F. In the mid 1980s, a number of Hind were seen with re-designed nose profiles and without the chin-mounted cannon, which gave rise to speculation about the possibility of the development of a specialist anti-helicopter version, designed to attack NATO attack helicopters – the 'marauding Hind'.

The Hind has been in action in a number of locations around the world where the Soviets are seeking to increase their influence, including Afghanistan whence the most interesting newsreel footage has originated. New tactics have been developed there against the Afghan tribesmen and, interestingly enough, it has been recently reported that more than 100 Hind have been lost to ground fire from 12.7mm, 14.5mm and 23mm guns, as well as a range of shoulder-held anti-aircraft missiles. As a result the Hinds fly higher and use modern counter-measures such as chaff and flares to decoy and confuse the rebel anti-aircraft systems.

The Hind remains in production, including the Mi-25 for export, but it may be superseded by 1990 with newer forms of attack helicopter, like the Mi-28 Havoc. The attack helicopter is, however, firmly established within the inventory of the Soviet and other Warsaw Pact nations, just as it is firmly established as a major threat to the NATO battlefield helicopters.

SOVIET ATTACK HELICOPTERS

Design Bureau	**Mil OKB**
Model	**Mi-2**
NATO Code Name	Hoplite
Service entry	1964
Engines	2 × Isotov GTD-350
Crew	1/2
Gross weight	3700kg (8157lb)
Max speed	113 knots (209km/h)
Range	237nm (440km)
Weapons	1 × 12.7mm or 23mm gun; 57mm rocket launchers

Design Bureau	**Mil OKB**
Model	**Mi-24**
NATO Code Name	Hind-A
Service entry	1972
Engines	2 × Isotov TV2-117A
Crew	2/3/4
Gross weight	8400kg (18519lb)
Max speed	157 knots (290km/h)
Range	173nm (320km)
Weapons	1 × 12.7mm gun; 4 × 57mm rocket launchers; 4 × Swatter anti-tank missiles

Design Bureau	**Mil OKB**
Model	**Mi-8**
NATO Code Name	Hip-E
Service entry	1970
Engines	2 × Isotov TV2-117A
Crew	2/3
Gross weight	12000kg (26455lb)
Max speed	140 knots (260km/h)
Range	251nm (465km)
Weapons	2 to 6 × Swatter anti-tank missiles; 57mm rocket launchers; 12.7mm or 23mm guns (in combination)

Design Bureau	**Mil OKB**
Model	**Mi-24**
NATO Code Name	Hind-D
Service entry	1976
Engines	2 × Isotov TV3-117
Crew	2/3
Gross weight	10000kg (22045lb)
Max speed	173 knots (320km/h)
Range	as Hind-A
Weapons	1 × 23mm cannon (or 1 × 12.7mm gun); 4 × 57mm rocket launchers; 4 × Swatter anti-tank missiles

Design Bureau	**Mil OKB**		Design Bureau	**Mil OKB**
Model	**Mi-24**		Model	**Mi-28**
NATO Code Name	Hind-E		NATO Code Name	Havoc
Service entry	1980		Service entry	1985
Engines	2 × Isotov TV3-117A		Engines	2 × TV4-117
Crew	2/3		Crew	2
Gross weight	10500kg (23148lb)		Gross weight	7100kg (15653lb)
Max speed	180 knots (333km/h)		Max speed	162 knots (300km/h)
Range	as Hind-A		Range	259nm (480km)
Weapons	1 × 23mm cannon; 4 × 57mm rocket launchers; 4 × Spiral anti-tank/air-to-air missiles		Weapons	1 × 23mm cannon; 16 × Spiral anti-tank/air-to-air missiles or 8 × air-to-air missiles

158. It was several years after the Mil Mi-8 had been introduced to service that the Soviet armed forces decided to attach hardpoints for weapons. All subsequent Mi-8, like the Hungarian Hip-C, were fitted with attachment points for weapons carriers, specifically the 57mm rocket launcher.

159. An unusually close and detailed view of a Polish Hip-C being rearmed during an exercise with Warsaw Pact forces. This helicopter is not fitted with IFF and the personal weapon of the soldier suggests a late 1960s picture recently re-released.

160. From the armed Hip concept, the Soviet Mil OKB (design bureau) brought the Mi-24 Hind-A into the arsenal (and the fears of most non-Soviet troops). The Hind-A was more of an assault helicopter than an attack type, but the formidable punch of 128 57mm rockets and the four AT-2 Swatter anti-tank missiles is impressive by any standards.

161. A close-up of the helicopter's rocket pods and the rails for the anti-tank missiles, taken as a Hind-A overflies the cameraman, probably during a parade in East Berlin or East Germany. Western analysts have not been able to identify all the bumps and bulges on the Hind.

▲160   ▼161

162. The use of touch-up here suggests that this tandem-seated Hind-D's formation number has been removed to prevent the exact location, time and date being identified by the Soviets. In other words, this picture was taken clandestinely. Note the cabin for assault troops which is used for ground equipment and spare ammunition in most of the Hind-D and E versions seen by Western observers. (US DoD)

163. A rather grainy, but worthwhile illustration of the Hind-D's nose, showing the gimbal-mounted 4-barrelled Gatling-type 12.7mm cannon, flanked by the all-weather radar guidance for the AT-2 Swatter missiles (port side), and the visual sensor pod (starboard) which contains low-light TV and forward-looking infra-red systems. Above the gun is the pitot tube for collecting air data for the helicopter's instruments.

164. The same helicopter as 162 and 163, showing the weapons stub wing with the permanently fitted UV-32 rocket launcher which contains 32 57mm rockets with a range of up to 5km (3 miles). These are used against tank and other vehicle targets, as well as troop concentrations. Outboard of the rocket launchers are the empty rails for the AT-2 Swatter.

162▲

163▲ 164▼

▲165   ▼166

165. Head-on view of the Hind-D which shows the weaponry and sensor suites to good effect. The pilot sits in the rear cockpit behind a glass windscreen which is capable of deflecting 23mm shells, and the gunner sits in front with the gunnery and weapon controls. It has been thought that there is an additional crew member, possibly an engineer, but it may be that he is only carried during detachment away from base.

166. This is traditional Hind country! The open plains of White Russia, the Caucasus and the Ukraine are treeless and generally devoid of cover, so that the Soviet forces have designed the Hind and engineered its tactics for assault rather than waiting in ambush Lynx-like. The Soviet air force would use the helicopters directly to support armoured thrusts along a very wide front. These four Hind were photographed during a missile assault' on Exercise 'Caucasus '85'. (TASS via Mike Gething)

167. All work and no play makes Ivan a dull boy. During Exercise 'Caucasus '85' an amateur folk-group performs for an army aviation unit. This is an interesting picture because it shows the Mi-6 Hook support helicopters (left) which transport the material for the Hind-D assault formations. (TASS via Mike Gething)

168. A Soviet Hind-D photographed off the coast of East Germany by US aircraft. The camouflage pattern is interesting, being sand-brown overall with mid-brown patterns, sky-blue underside, yellow formation numbers and the traditional yellow-outlined Red Star. (US DoD via Mike Gething)

168▼

◄169   170▲

169. Frequently seen on the border between Federal Germany and Czechoslovakia, the Hind-D patrol the border in parallel with the US Army Cobras and unarmed German police helicopters. This Czech Hind-D is painted in two-tone brown with a sky-blue underside and black or yellow 'danger tail rotor' markings. Note that there are only two 57mm rocket launchers being carried, although the standard 12.7mm gun is probably fully loaded and armed. (W W Duck)

170. In Afghanistan there has been continual Press coverage of the use of chemical weapons against the Afghan rebels who oppose the Soviet invasion. In April 1986, the US DoD released this artist's impression of a chemical spraying attachment to the standard Hind-D helicopter, with the tanks taking the place of the UV-32 rocket launchers. The second Hind in this view is providing the spraying helicopter with top cover.

171. One of the first views of what many observers feel was the latest Hind-E version of the Russian attack helicopter, but the absence of AT-6 Grail guidance equipment and launch rails, as well as the lack of 23mm cannon rather suggest that this a Hind-D in a training version. The Russians have never divulged how their helicopter variants are identified. This picture was apparently taken in August 1984 at the Syzran Air Force Academy. (TASS via Whitton Press)

171▼

Future Concepts
and Developments

For many nations, the idea of an attack helicopter is out of the question, and for others the need is for a dedicated highly effective machine. There are, therefore, several important future concepts and developments which will shape the development of the attack helicopter during the next few decades.

Night operations. For many years it has been the dream of every battlefield commander to be able to call upon attack helicopters at any time during the 24-hour battle. Until recently, it has not been possible to fight attack helicopters at night, although, with the use of night vision goggles, it has been easy enough to navigate along known routes from place to place. One of the keys to night fighting is the forward-looking infra-red system which uses a thermal-imaging module to sense differences in heat sources – people, tanks and man-made objects stand out from the background. Types like the AH-64A Apache, now coming into full-scale service, and future attack helicopters will be capable of adverse weather and night operation.

Cockpit management. Because the workload of the attack helicopter pilot is growing yearly, several nations have begun developing mission management systems which not only tidy-up the cockpit but also allow for the possibility of the singleman cockpit by the year 2000. The US Army's LHX (Light Helicopter Experiment) programme has been developing since 1983, on the strength of the expertize within US and some European avionics houses to develop systems which will allow a single pilot to fly close to the ground, in all weathers, fight the perceived threats, carry out his task and return safely to base with a helicopter capable of being used again within minutes. The US Army believes that attack helicopters should be used around the clock to provide a viable and flexible counter to enemy tank movements at any time, therefore it needs more than one person per helicopter seat, hence the interest in single-pilot helicopters.

Smaller nations also need management systems that will reduce pilot workload thus increasing safety, because much of the pilot fatigue of an attack helicopter pilot is taken away. The basis of such systems are computers and microprocessors which store and display information as required. Eventually, voice actuation and control will be possible and there could even be self-healing systems which if hit could repair themselves.

Weapons. Attack helicopters now carry anti-attack missiles, cannon, machine-guns and/or rockets as a matter of course, but there still may not be enough guided weapons in the NATO inventories to defeat the perceived Warsaw Pact armour forces should there ever be war again in Central Europe. To counter this imbalance, the US Army has completed trials with the Hellfire-armed Black Hawk tactical transport helicopter.

The idea of the fire support Black Hawk carrying sixteen laser-designated Hellfires (but not having the means to designate the target) is to supplement the

◀**172.** In the attack role, the BK 117 is equally effective at night as by day, using the infra-red module in the mast-mounted sight which is capable of launching and tracking the HOT missiles while the gunner could wear night vision goggles, linked to the Lucas 12.7mm gun.

Apache force, with designation being provided by the OH-58D Aeroscout or the Apache itself. Other schemes, so far unadopted, have included the use of rocket-carrying Chinook and lightweight 'suicide' remotely piloted helicopters.

The next generation of anti-tank weapon, the so-called third-generation missile, will have a lock-on after launch capability which will enable the next generation of helicopters, like HAC and PAH-2, to operate from stand-off ranges outside the defensive fire zone of armoured formations. Britain, France and Federal Germany have combined to develop Trigat for this role and it is thought that Rockwell will develop the Hellfire concept further to give the US Army a third-generation weapon.

Air-to-air. Another area where new weapons are being developed is in air-to-air combat between two or more helicopters or between a helicopter and a fixed-wing aircraft. With the continuous advances in Soviet anti-helicopter weaponry, including the Hind-E's 23mm cannon and the dual role laser-guided AT-6 Spiral missile, air-to-air operations have been taken very seriously by NATO.

In the United States, training exercises have now been undertaken with a variety of helicopters including the MBB BK 117, Bell AH-1S Cobra, the Bell OH-58 Kiowa, the Sikorsky S-76 and UH-60A Black Hawk. New weapons for helicopters include the AIM-9 Sidewinder air-to-air missile for the AH-1W SuperCobra, and the Stinger for the OH-58D Aéroscout. In France, Thomson-CSF and Crouzet have developed helicopter gun sights for firing cannon against ground and air targets.

The new generation LHX will be armed with a 20mm or 30mm cannon, linked to a helmet-mounted display and able to engage rapidly moving targets; these helicopters will be armed with air-to-air missiles.

Small nations. With the cost of attack helicopter programmes escalating to the point where even the largest nations are finding it nearly impossible to finance the cost, it is not surprising that smaller nations are looking for ways to obtain an attack capability without the high cost. In Romania, the state aircraft factory has re-configured the Alouette III into a tandem-seat helicopter called the IAR-317 Airfox. The helicopter is armed with AT-2 Swatter missiles and rocket launchers.

South Africa, faced with an arms embargo, has completely re-designed the Alouette III to include a powerful cannon under the nose and an interesting tandem-seating arrangement. The prototype first flew in 1984 and it seems that the project will be developed further.

Chile is endeavouring to develop the MBB BO 105 into an attack helicopter, armed with a locally produced gun. The gun has definitely returned to the attack helicopter scene.

Even in the United States there are companies eager to develop very cost-effective attack helicopters for the Third World market. One example is the Aerodyne Hornet which shows a lineage stretching back to the Bell 47.

Advanced designs. The next generation of European attack helicopter is already taking shape. Agusta's A129 has already flown in Italy, while the Franco-German consortium called Eurocopter is building a series of two attack helicopters (France's HAC and Germany's PAH-2) and the HAP escort and anti-helicopter helicopter for the French ALAT. These helicopters will be armed with third-generation weapons and will be capable of operating day and night against most perceived threats.

In the United States there have been several advanced programmes. The US Army is engaged on the replacement of its ageing light transport and attack helicopters with a new family under the LHX banner. Initially several revolutionary designs were studied, including tilt-rotor, advancing blade concept and X-Wing. Eventually, the conventional helicopter won on the grounds of least technical risk in development.

The major helicopter manufacturers in the US have teamed together for LHX – Boeing-Sikorsky's FirstTeam and Bell-McDonnell Douglas' SuperTeam – to provide prototypes for the LHX-SCAT (SCout-ATtack) and the LHX-U (Utility) versions which will replace most of the UH-1 Huey, OH-58 Kiowa and AH-1 Cobra airframes in the next one and a half decades. At least 500 LHX helicopters will be needed before the year 2005, so this US programme is attracting considerable attention.

The US Marine Corps will replace its medium helicopter force with the Bell-Boeing V-22A Osprey tilt-rotor from about 1993, partly using expertize developed in the Bell XV-15 programme. Now it is possible that the Marines will require an escort tilt-rotor to protect the V-22 during an assault, particularly against enemy fighters and close air support aircraft. No funding has yet been given for the attack version of the tilt-rotor, but many commentators believe that it is only a matter of time. That will put a completely different complexion on the attack helicopter scene.

FUTURE AMERICAN PROGRAMMES

Programme	**LHX (Light Helicopter Experiment)**
Sponsor	**US Army**
Competitors	Boeing-Sikorsky & Bell-McDonnell Douglas
Service entry	1992–95
Role	Scout and attack
Crew	1
Gross weight	3629kg (8000lb)
Max speed	170 knots (315km/h)
Range	300nm (556km)
Weapons	Hellfire anti-tank missiles; Stinger air-to-air missiles; 70mm rocket launchers

FUTURE SOVIET PROGRAMMES

Design Bureau	**Kamov OKB**
Model	**Ka-29 (?)**
NATO Code Name	Hokum
Service entry	(awaited)
Engines	2 × TV4-117
Crew	2
Gross weight	unknown
Max speed	190 knots (352km/h)
Range	270nm (500km)
Weapons	1 × 23mm cannon and unspecified missiles

Design Bureau	**Mil OKB**
Model	**Mi-32**
NATO Code Name	unknown (tilt-rotor)
Service entry	project only
Engines	2 × new type
Crew	2
Gross weight	unknown
Max speed	300 knots (556km/h)
Range	300nm (556km)
Weapons	new- generation gun and missiles

173. Special trials were carried out in the Aérospatiale SA 361H helicopter to carry HOT anti-tank missiles, a standard day sight (mounted in the roof) and a nose-mounted FLIR for night operations. The design, including the faired-over missile launchers, proved to be adequate for attack tasks if a little ungainly. (Euromissile)

174. After the SA 361H, trials moved to the SA 365 Dauphin 2 with its tricycle undercarriage and twin-engined safety. By 1982, the French had started to perfect tactics for night operations, but although there was an army requirement, funding for full development was not forthcoming. (Euromissile)

175. For fighting at night the FLIR system can be used, but for ordinary navigation and flying, the pilot is equipped with a pair of image-intensifying night vision goggles (pilot on left). In this picture, the co-pilot/gunner is using the roof-mounted sight. The helicopter is again the SA 365N Dauphin 2. (Euromissile)

176. The view through the FLIR of the SA 361H. Although monochrome only, the display gives a clear indication of the running soldiers and the armoured vehicle. Note the APC's engine is running; the intensity of the heat is shown by the brightness of the heat source (white as against grey). The missile aimer would use the cross hairs to keep the HOT on target, aiming for the APC which is readily identifiable despite the fact that it is cloaked in darkness.

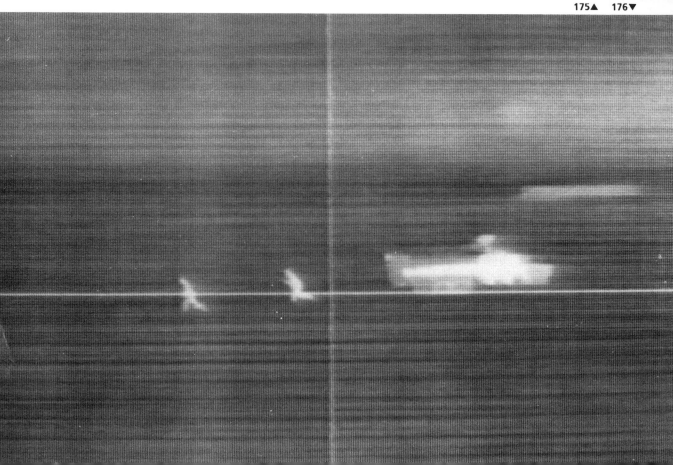

▲177 ▼178

177,178. In 1985, Boeing Helicopters began to fly the first of the US Army funded Advanced Rotorcraft Technology Integration testbeds, using an Agusta A 109A Mk II helicopter as the platform. The helicopter was re-configured for two pilots, one as a safety pilot in the front right-hand seat and the other – the test pilot – in a specially designed pilot's seat directly behind the cockpit. The test pilot uses cathode ray tubes (CRT) mounted in the centre section with a camera on the airframe. Instead of using visual cues and references, the outside scene is shown on camera and the pilot flies using the pictures. (Boeing)

179. In an attempt to make the smaller attack helicopter more effective, McDonnell Douglas Helicopter Company has installed a cockpit management system in the 530MG Defender. Information is fed from normal data acquisition equipment, backed up and supplemented by a FLIR (under the nose) and the Hughes Aircraft mast-mounted sight.

180,181. These pictures show the difference in cockpit arrays for the 500MD (180) and the new 530MG (181). In the 500MD Defender there are conventional analogue displays for all the flight functions, including weapons engagement and navigation. The chin-mounted M65 TOW weapon sight takes up a large amount of the left-hand side of the cockpit. In the 530MG, Racal Avionics have supplied CRT for all functions (with only stand-by instruments), the switches have been simplified and the TOW mast-mounted sight equipment folds away because the direct view optics have been replaced by TV monitoring. Each CRT can also display the FLIR and MMS imagery.

179 ▲

180▲   181▼

182. MBB have gone part way by the road with the BK 117A-3M demonstrator which shows various displays and management systems for the modern multi-role helicopter. In this view, the radios (bottom centre) can be selected by using touch pads and the flight critical information is shown on bar displays in front of the pilot. Other interesting systems include a radar warning receiver display (top left).

183. Developed to assist the Apache and Cobra fire teams in the event of an armoured assault on US or allied positions, this specially modified UH-60A Black Hawk can carry sixteen Rockwell Hellfire missiles on its external stores carriers which are usually used for carrying overload fuel tanks to allow the helicopter to self-deploy to Korea or Europe. The Black Hawk lacks any laser designation equipment for the Hellfires, but the weapon-carrying role is an easy modification.

▲182   ▼183

184. In 1984, the Westland Lynx AH 1 was modified to test fire the Hellfire missile during the clearance trials for the Lynx-3 and the possible use of the missile by the British Army as an interim fit before the Trigat system is ready for service. A ground laser designator was used to aim the missiles which were fired on a range in Norway. Additions to the missile launcher include cameras for the tests.

185. The advent of the Mil Mi-28 Havoc in 1985 has led to an increased awareness of the potential of the modern attack helicopter to undertake air-to-air as well as anti-tank attack operations. This artist's impression shows the Mi-28 armed with a 23mm turret, eight modern generation laser-guided anti-tank missiles (inboard) and four air-to-air missiles (SA-14 modified) on the outboard weapons stub. The helicopter is reported to have been tested in Afghanistan and to have entered production in 1986. (US DoD)

184▲   185▼

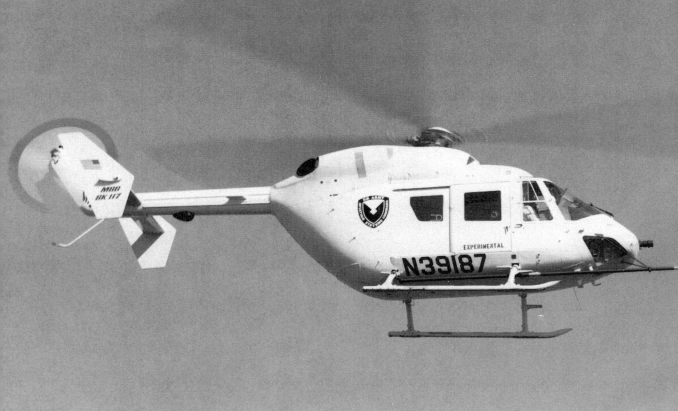

186. Among the helicopters which the US Army's Aviation Systems Command is testing for air-to-air combat abilities is the BK 117A-1 which has been flying in experimental form since early 1986 at Patuxent River, Maryland. Note the data-collection probes and the forward-facing camera. (Bob Metzger/MBB)

187. The first helicopter to enter operational service with the AIM-9 Sidewinder missile as a weapon option is the Bell AH-1W SuperCobra which entered USMC service in March 1986. Besides the 20mm gun in the chin turret, the helicopter can carry two Sidewinders on the stub wings, and trials are being carried out to determine the best tactics to use with the weapon. (Bell)

188. From France comes the Crouzet helicopter pilot's sight for attack helicopters engaged in strafing ground targets with missiles and guns, or for air-to-air combat with other helicopters and even certain fixed-wing types which might wander onto the battlefield. This test installation is shown in the Aérospatiale Gazelle. (Crouzet)

189. Honeywell has developed a helmet-mounted sight system for use in attack helicopters and presumably for the forthcoming LHX programme in the air-to-air role as well as air-to-ground. The pilot sees the target's image in the visor and is given launch cues and parameters. As he turns his head the gun/missile system will train with him and the constraints data is updated.

188▲ 189▼

▲190

▲191   ▼192

190. An artist's impression of LHX-SCAT engaging a Hind during an air-to-air battle of the future. The LHX is equipped with a gun in a gimbal-mounted turret and the single pilot is using a helmet-mounted sight to acquire and destroy the target. (Boeing-Sikorsky)

191,192. In Chile, the local armaments industry has been developing the BO 105 into a light attack helicopter, armed with a locally produced gun (192) and rocket launchers. There were rumours of the helicopter at the FIDA show in Santiago in 1984 and this model was shown there in 1986. No decision has been taken on production, but there is a requirement from the Chilean Army for an attack helicopter.

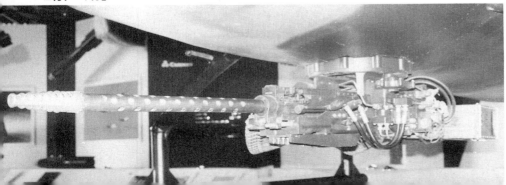

193. In Romania, the Alouette III (which is still in production there) has come in for development by the state helicopter factory, IAR, which has developed a tandem-seat attack helicopter from the basic French airframe. The new helicopter, shown at Paris in 1985, has been named the IAR 317 Airfox and is armed with Soviet-built missiles and rockets. (J. M. de Casteja)

194. Called the Alpha, this Alouette III derivative has been developed by the South Africa aircraft and defence industry for future bush war conflicts in that troubled area. The helicopter first flew in 1984 and was shown off in March 1986. It is of tandem configuration and is armed with a 20mm cannon; it is presumed to have entered production. (SAAF)

195,196. Designed around the Bell 47 and developed by the remotely piloted vehicle manufacturers, Aerodyne Systems Engineering, the Hornet is designed to fulfil the needs of smaller nations seeking an effective but cheap attack helicopter. To be used in areas of low intensity, such as border security and policing, the helicopter is armed with rocket launchers.

197. In model form the HAC-3G is an interesting third-generation attack helicopter development. It has been designed by Aérospatiale and MBB under the joint auspices of Eurocopter. It is armed with the Trigat missile, using a mast-mounted sight for

▲195 ▼196

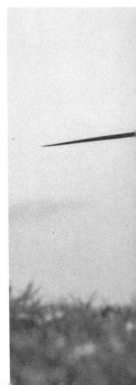

attack acquisition and a pilot's night vision sensor on the nose to assist navigation and night flying. The HAC will be night/day and adverse weather capable; it should enter service in 1995/6.

198. Using the same basic airframe, the Federal German Army is seeking to develop the PAH-2. Note the difference in the configuration as compared to the HAC (197). For example, it has no mast-mounted sight, using instead the TADS/PNVS system of the Apache. In terms of armament, it carries the same Trigat anti-tank missiles, but is also armed with air-to-air missiles at the end of the stub wings.

197▲ 198▼

▲199

199. Shown at Hanover Air Fair in 1986, the engineering mock-up of the PAH-2 shows a large helicopter with tandem seating, the pilot in the rear seat and the co-pilot/gunner in the forward position.

200. One of Sikorsky's advanced ideas was the ABC – advancing blade concept – which gave greater speed than a conventional helicopter because the contra-rotating rotors effectively did away with retreating blade stall, the speed restricting factor of a modern helicopter.

▼200

201,202. When the US Army commenced trials for a new light scout and attack helicopter (SCAT), contenders included the Bell Advanced Tilt-rotor or BAT (201) which was shown in mock-up form in 1985. The air vehicle is single-pilot with a V-tail; the engines rotate to give lift and/or forward speed, allowing the vertical take-off performance of a helicopter and the forward speed of turboprop aircraft. Boeing introduced a scheme for a tilt-rotor (202) with a folding mast-mounted sight, cannon armament and a single pilot. Neither was selected.

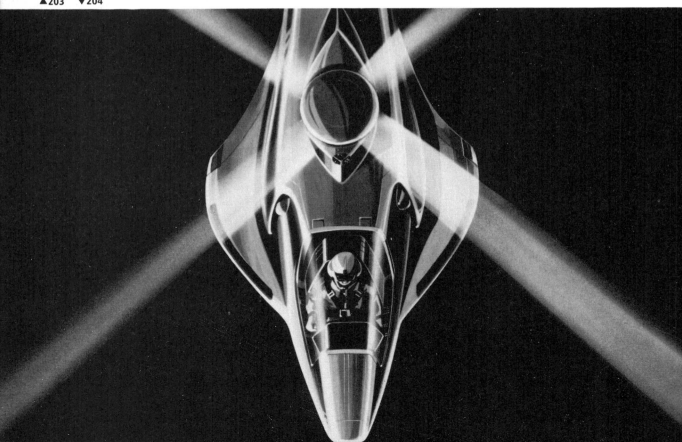

203,204. The shape of things to come. Bell-McDonnell Douglas's SuperTeam LHX entrant in artist's impressional form. The tail area was not included with the original illustration because it is a possible competition winning factor – LHX might be notar (no tail rotor) or fenestron (ducted tail rotor). The overall concept is single pilot and modern technology.

205. An early McDonnell Douglas version of the LHX proposal which clearly shows the single-pilot fighter aircraft style of the attack helicopter of the future. The weapons are faired into the airframe to reduce drag and increase reliability. About 5,000 of these helicopters (or the eventual winning design) will be required by the year 2000 to replace the US Army's current fleet of light helicopters.

206,207. Hunting on the future battlefield. The Sikorsky concept of a fenestron-equipped, single-pilot attack helicopter. Two of these are moving into an ambush position (206) from which to engage enemy tanks with a new generation anti-tank missile (207). The helicopters in the picture would then be engaged with the gun or with air-to-air missiles; it is possible that the next generation of helicopter-borne missile will be jointly air-to-air/air-to-ground.

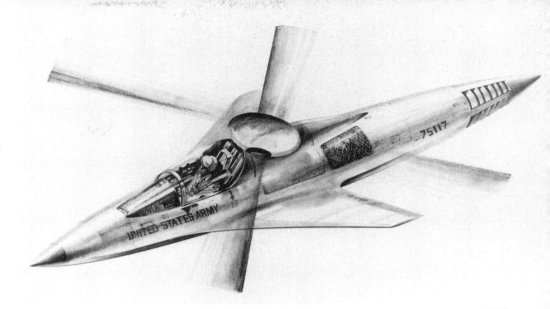

205 ▲

206▲ 207▼

▲208

208. The US forces have proceeded with the development of a large tilt-rotor for future air transportation, replacing the USMC's medium helicopters, some US Army and USAF special operations aircraft, and for naval duties with the USN. The forerunner was the Bell XV-15 development aircraft, seen here in trials over the Arizona desert and showing its tilt-rotors in a semi-hovering low-medium speed mode.

▼209

209. An artist's cutaway of the future tilt-rotor escort air vehicle for future amphibious operations, combining the role of attack helicopter, fleet fighter and strike fighter. The armament includes air-to-ground and air-to-air missiles as well as a 30mm cannon. Note the two-man crew needed for such complex operations.

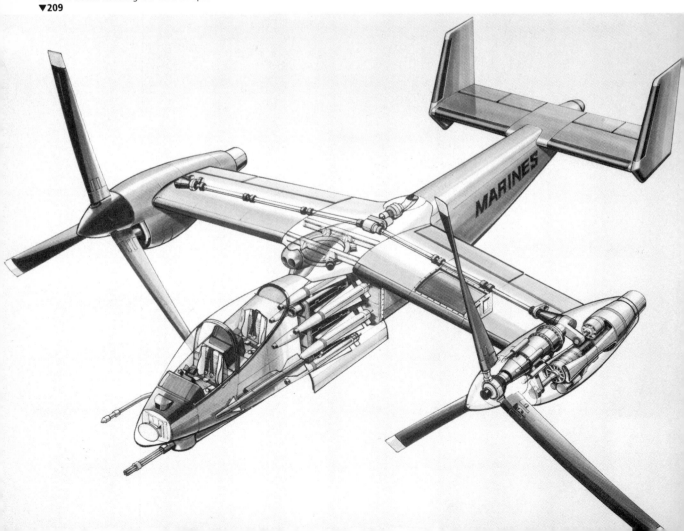

APPENDIX
World Distribution of
Armed Helicopters

Country	No.	Type	Country	No.	Type
Afghanistan	75	Mi-8/Mi-24	Guinea Republic	none	
Albania	none		Guyana	none	
Algeria	28	Mi-24/25	Haiti	none	
Angola	27	Gazelle/Mi-25	Honduras	7	S-76A
Argentina	none		Hong Kong	none	
Australia	none		Hungary	42	Mi-8/Mi-24
Austria	none		Iceland	none	
Bahrain	none		India	30	Chetak
Bangladesh	12	Mi-8	Indonesia	none	
Belgium	none		Iran	20	SeaCobra
Bolivia	12	MD 500M	Iraq	60	Mi-24/MD 500/
Botswana	2	AS 350L			Gazelle
Brazil	none		Israel	52	Cobra/MD 500
Brunei	none		Italy	70	A109/A129
Bulgaria	18	Mi-8/Mi-24	Ivory Coast	none	
Burma	none		Jamaica	none	
Burundi	none		Japan	75	Cobra
Cameroon	none		Jordan	24	Cobra
Canada	none		Kenya	30	MD 500
Central African			Korea North	30	MD 500
Republic	none		Korea South	27	Cobra
Chad	none		Kuwait	25	Gazelle
Chile	none		Laos	10	Mi-24
China (PR)	none		Lebanon	4	Gazelle
Colombia	16	MD 500M/500MG	Lesotho	none	
Congo	none		Liberia	none	
Costa Rica	none		Libya	76	Mi-8/Mi-24/Gazelle
Cuba	32	Mi-8/Mi-24	Malagasy		
Czechoslovakia	50	Mi-8/Mi-24	Republic	none	
Denmark	none		Malawi	1	AS 350L
Djibouti	none		Malaysia	none	
Dominican			Mali	none	
Republic	none		Mauritania	none	
Ecuador	5	Gazelle	Mexico	none	
Egypt	160	Gazelle/Mi-8/Cobra	Monaco	none	
Eire	none		Mongolia	3	Mi-8
Ethiopia	12	Mi-8/Mi-24	Morocco	48	Gazelle/MD 500
Finland	none		Mozambique	20	Mi-8/Mi-25
France	180	Gazelle/Alouette III	Nepal	none	
Gabon	7	Gazelle/AS 350	Netherlands	none	
Germany East	60	Mi-8/Mi-24	New Zealand	none	
Germany West	207	BO 105P	Nicaragua	20	Mi-8/Mi-24
Ghana	none		Nigeria	none	
Greece	none		Norway	none	
Guatemala	none		Oman	none	
Guinea-Bissau	1	Gazelle	Pakistan	22	Cobra